WHAT MAKES WINNERS WIN?

The Five Attributes That Will Make You a Success in Selling

CHARLES W. HITZEMANN

PGI PRESS

Library of Congress Cataloging-in-Publication Data

Hitzemann, Charles W.
        What makes winners win? - the five attributes that will make you a success in selling.

Catalog Number: 98-91558

ISBN 0-9665066-0-X

Printed in the United States of America

CONTENTS

Acknowledgment

This book was written because of the generosity and wise counsel of H. Gordon Bethards, a master salesman and teacher who coached scores of men and women to be winners in the sales profession.

As my sales manager in the beginning years of my selling career, Gordon taught me skills that have continually proven their value to this day. As a loyal friend and trusted confidant throughout the years, his experience, insight, and energy are a source of continuing inspiration and learning.

Gordon's stories, freely shared then and now, are a vital part of this book.

Chuck Hitzemann
Smith Mountain Lake, Virginia

INTRODUCTION

My sales career began at age twenty-seven following four and one-half years service as an officer in the United States Army. I worked for Gordon Bethards, a former Army Master Sergeant, who was now a master salesman, sales manager, and teacher. Gordon believed that training was an essential ingredient for success and under his watchful eye, I began a journey to learn and apply skills to effectively and profitably create and keep delighted customers. As a sales manager and professional selling skills coach, I have had the opportunity to help men and women grow in the mastery of sales and I enjoy seeing many examples of outstanding salesmanship in everyday application.

This book is about selling skills -- some I learned, some I developed, and others I observed. These skills are embodied in the five attributes that will make you a success in selling:

1. **technical knowledge**
2. **sincere interest in people**
3. **customer focused selling**
4. **drive to contact many customers and prospects**
5. **organization**

About The Word "Product"

Throughout this book the word "product" also means

"service." Indeed, many providers of services refer to their service as a product. The same is true with intangibles such as insurance, financial services, stocks and bonds, or even charities and ideas. No matter what you sell, when you see the word "product" think of your product, service, policy, contract, or whatever you call it. It makes no difference whether you are selling tangible or intangible products, the five attributes have the same value.

"This Doesn't Apply To Me"

You can learn from those who sell things that are not identical to what you sell. One of the most helpful books I ever bought was *How I Raised Myself From Failure To Success In Selling* by Frank Bettger, an insurance salesman. I never sold insurance, but I found the techniques Bettger wrote about were universal in application. The details may differ between what you sell and what I sell, but the basic principles are the same and you can adapt the techniques to fit your situation.

Do yourself a favor and don't fall into the trap of saying to yourself, "This doesn't apply to me." Read the entire book and then decide. You need only one new idea to make it worth your time. You'll find that one new idea, maybe more.

Selling Is A Wonderful Profession

Be proud of what you do. Selling is a wonderful way to spend your life. If you are now a salesperson you will find useful ideas in **WHAT MAKES WINNERS WIN?** to increase your income and your satisfaction. If you are not now a salesperson, you may decide to become one. As a sales representative you can help other people acquire products that will benefit them in many ways or maybe just make them feel good. That's what salespeople do.

CHAPTER 1

TECHNICAL KNOWLEDGE

Summary: In-depth knowledge of products and services, both yours and competitive, is vital to selling success.

During one period in my years as a sales manager, our twelve-person sales team sold herbicides, fungicides and insecticides to control weeds, diseases and insects in crops. It was common to hire farm-reared men and women with at least a bachelors degree in some discipline of agriculture for the selling job. Most members of the team had master's degrees; two held doctorates. And then there was Harold. Harold was a high school graduate.

Harold had grown up in the citrus groves and had followed his father through the trees since the time he could walk. Following high school, he enrolled in college, but after a few months decided campus life was not for him. Returning home, he began selling products to citrus producers, and became very successful.

Harold was one of the most effective salespeople I have ever known. Although he had not earned a college degree, he possessed extraordinary knowledge and wisdom gained over the years as he worked amid the orange and grapefruit groves. With all his practical experience, Harold had catalogued everything in his mind about citrus. He had farmed and on top of that he knew all the technicalities.

When I met Harold he had been in his territory for several years and was widely known as a bottomless well of accurate, reliable technical knowledge. The dealers and growers ran after him. He was on the go from dawn to dark, and often on Saturdays and Sundays, too. "Please come to a block of trees that are looking bad," or "My growers have some weeds coming through which they can't identify and are at a loss about what to do," were typical messages he'd hear on his answering machine.

Harold gave his time unselfishly. He was a "partner in production"; an expert who knew the business better than anyone else.

Did he sell our products? Yes. He sold huge quantities. His sales results were not because he used pressure tactics, but because people trusted him and, in a large part, bought because they valued his technical assistance. Customers will do that -- they'll give their business to the seller who helps them the most. Many people would never even classify Harold as a salesman, but he sold tons of products and it was largely because of his technical knowledge.

A Slasher Story

While visiting in the car on one of our first trips together in my sales territory, Gordon told me about an experience as a beginning salesperson for the DuPont Company. One of his products was a "warp-size" for nylon. Warp-size is a coating applied on the lengthwise threads of fabric (the warp) before the weaver places it in a loom. The coating protects the fabric from abrasion as the bobbin whips back and forth with the crosswise threads (the weft) to weave the fabric.

The operators apply the coating to the warp in a machine called a slasher. The slasher consists of a bath containing the coating solution, a series of drying cylinders, and a beam to rewind the treated warp.

The warp unwinds from a beam at the front end of the slasher, passes through the bath, over and around the series of drying cylinders, and rewinds on a beam at the back end of the slasher. Then the operators transfer the beam with the coated warp to a loom for weaving.

Several variables are important in operating the slasher: a) the temperature of the coating solution, b) the temperatures in each of the five drying cylinders, and c) the speed at which the warp passes through the solution bath and over the drying cylinders.

The product Gordon sold, an acrylic resin, was about 10-times more costly than the corn starch normally used as a warp-size on cotton goods. However, starch was not giving the nylon threads adequate protection. The textile mills were willing to try anything else, however expensive, if it would do the job.

Gordon made the initial round of the mills with the new coating, explained in detail how to use it, and took an introductory order on most of the calls.

As he started the second round of visits, he found very discontented customers. The product, they said, wasn't working. He was baffled because extensive research data had demonstrated the product would work, if properly used. Gordon realized, however, that he had never seen a slasher. "If I knew how to operate a slasher," he said to himself, "I'll bet I could make the product work."

He promptly scheduled a visit with the technical superintendent of a large mill in Virginia. Instead of talking about his product, Gordon quizzed the superintendent about slasher operation. In a few minutes the superintendent said, "Come on, we're running your stuff in the slasher right now, let's go look at it."

With the background his research chemists had given him, it was easy to identify the problem. Gordon, himself, had graduated from the University of Delaware with a degree in organic chemistry and had five years of laboratory experience with DuPont. The temperatures were all wrong. The customer was using the same temperatures in the bath and in the drying cylinders they had always used for the starch based product. The DuPont product would only work under a totally different set of temperature relationships. Although Gordon had explained that vital information on the initial calls, the mill operators had uniformly ignored it.

Over the objections of the operators running the slasher, Gordon adjusted the temperatures and the through-put speed to the levels he knew were correct. For the next several hours they ran four beams of nylon warp through the slasher.

As each beam came off the slasher it went to a loom for weaving. By the end of the day this mill was producing satisfactory fabric for the first time. The results delighted the mill personnel from the general manager on down.

Gordon was now a slasher expert. It didn't take long for the word to get around.

On To Another Mill

Just two days later, Gordon received an emergency summons from another mill, owned and operated by the same company. It was a mill where he had tried three times to visit with the technical director. On each occasion he had been rebuffed with "We know what we're doing." This time the message was different. "We heard from our sister mill that you know how to run a slasher. Please come help us," was their plea.

When he arrived, Gordon found this mill was weaving ninety-five percent second-grade nylon fabric -- fabric with many defects. Since second-grade fabric sold for much less than first-grade fabric, the executives of the company were putting considerable pressure on the mill to do something about it.

With the technical superintendent at his side, Gordon took charge of the slasher operation and trained three shifts of operators in proper temperature controls and speed. When he left the mill, after an uninterrupted stint of thirty-six hours, they were weaving ninety-five percent first-grade fabric. The technical and production staffs were ecstatic. At that point Gordon thought he probably could have had the president's job, had he asked for it.

His intimate knowledge of his product, coupled with his newly acquired experience in slasher operation, were the resources Gordon combined to produce a delighted customer.

Advice and Consent

Hanley-Wood, Inc, publishes a trade magazine titled, *ProSales*. The *ProSales* audiences are the retail dealers and wholesale distributors of building materials. A few years ago, the magazine published an article titled "Advice and Consent," written by Rich Binsacca.

"Consultative selling may not be new, but it's still rare," is the subtitle of the article. Here is the first two-thirds of that article:

Be Prepared

Every Thursday at 11 a.m. for the past three and a half years, Rick Quaintance and Jack Ely have met to discuss the home building business, specifically that of Ideal Suburban Homes, where Ely is the construction manager. For three hours, the pair look over blueprints, talk about the week winding down, draw up a schedule for next week, and review the progress of the 50 or so homes Ideal has going up at any given time.

Meetings like this are common between a builder and his superintendents, but Quaintance isn't on the Ideal payroll. Rather, he is an outside salesperson for the Wickes Lumber yard in Fort Wayne, Ind., Ideal's primary supplier of building products. More than that, Quaintance is a consultant, confidant, and advisor to Ely and about 30 other accounts within a 75-mile radius of the store. His goal is to become a trusted, even invaluable, member of the building team.

Consultative selling isn't new to the pro sales business but isn't commonplace either. It involves selling construction expertise as much as product. It's hard work. But it often results in a client relationship that transcends the bottom line. "It's almost like being another employee of the customer's company," says Quaintance, who has practiced this sales philosophy for eight years.

Twelve years ago, Quaintance was driving a delivery truck for Wickes. Today, he's still driving, only now it's a pickup with a cellular phone. He visits job sites daily to inspect framing, note mistakes or unfinished work, take measurements, and update delivery schedules. "I realize that to be successful, you have to go out of your way and do what the competition isn't," says Quaintance.

That's often simply a matter of being prepared. Quaintance attributes a large part of his success to preparation. He retains the blueprints to every house built by his clients, and he continually reviews them to anticipate customer schedules and material needs. He confirms these needs through regular meetings with supers and framers. "I know what stage all the jobs are in," he says. "I know how fast the framers can go and when they'll need the next load."

While Quaintance studies blueprints, he doesn't always trust them. Subcontractors change things. So do homeowners. That's why once a house is framed and ready for drywall, Quaintance always measures for interior doors, windows, cabinets, vanities, and countertops, noting deviations from builder's specifications.

Quaintance willingly works with the builder's sub to schedule delivery. "I coordinate the schedule," he says, sounding more like a superintendent than a salesperson. The service permits managers like Ely to concentrate on the big picture -- coordinating the overall progress of the job. "I couldn't handle the 50 to 60 units we have going in various stages without that kind of assistance," says Ely.

Ideal, which builds about 130 units a year, rewards Quaintance and Wickes with annual purchases of about $1.5 million. Ely explains his allegiance to Quaintance: "He's familiar with our products and how we build. He's as important to us as any subcontractor."

Diligence has earned Quaintance a certain trust. Customers call for his design opinion and count on him to hunt for new products that save money without sacrificing value. In return they give him the opportunity to sell a variety of high-margin products -- not just lumber. "I don't think you could just come in and replace me," he says.

Quaintance is so involved in construction that he can catch problems before they happen. On one occasion, Graber Homes, based in Auburn, Ind., another of his accounts, put a bathtub less than 5 feet from a window. Quaintance saw the code violation at the blueprint stage and ordered safety glass. When the builder had trouble passing inspection, Quaintance provided proof from the glass manufacturer that the window had safety glass, and the house passed.

Prior to the big run up in lumber prices this past spring, Quaintance suggested that Graber add a contingency clause to its contracts to compensate for the uncertain lumber market. "That way, if prices increased, it could be tacked on at the end of the job," he says. Graber took the advice and saved thousands of dollars when prices still had not receded by March.

That kind of service has put money in Quaintance's pocket as well. When he took over the account, Graber was spending $60,000 a year with Wickes. Now the builder spends $1.2 million a year there.

The best salespeople know that their success depends on strong support back at the yard, and Quaintance is no exception. He relies on an inside sales staff to take care of his clients when he's on the road or can't be reached and to process the special orders he writes up. The teamwork has paid off. In the 12 years since Quaintance started driving delivery trucks, Wickes' Fort Wayne store has increased sales ten-fold to about $16 million a year.

Building Reputations

For 20 years Clint Olden sold building products to big developers in southern Virginia -- multifamily and large tract projects were his forte. Then, about four years ago, his company was folded into Carolina Builders, based in Raleigh, North Carolina. Carolina Builders wanted to concentrate on smaller, custom builders.

To some salespeople, these are different customers with an entirely different set of service priorities. Olden doesn't think so. He was able to apply the same consultative sales philosophy to his new account that had worked with his old ones. "If I tell a customer something is going to be done, it is," he says. "I built a reputation on that."

Olden works out of a store in Newport News. Twenty-five miles away, his friend and one-time assistant, Buzz Sawyer, operates with the same philosophy out of a Carolina Builders store in Norfolk, with much the same results. "There's no such thing as just selling and walking off," says Sawyer. "In a large sense you have to be partners with the builder."

In Olden's case, that often means suggesting products to help customers execute designs. He meets with builders on site to go over the elevations, looking closely at relationships among the windows and other architectural elements. "They expect me to provide input, like whether to use a double or triple window on the front of the house," says Olden.

The salesman is typically called in while the frame can still be changed to accommodate his suggestions. But Olden's larger clients will even ask for his input during the design phase, when he makes suggestions based on *preliminary plans. "They'll ask me, `What can we do here to keep costs down and still get a better value?'" he says.*

Some services are required by builders of all sizes, such as smooth deliveries. So Olden routinely sets up preconstruction meetings with the builder and job superintendent. The group determines an initial schedule for the job and pencils in when deliveries are likely to be needed.

But custom builders often have special needs. They may call on Olden to investigate products that Carolina doesn't stock. They may also want to see the product used in construction before they'll agree to the spec. So Olden often takes customers on road trips to check out products.

Fortunately, Carolina Builders Supply boasts an extensive network of stores and its own milling productions services. "It's a large enough company that I can find a product or get information in-house and quickly," says Sawyer. Adds Olden, "With our millwork capabilities, I can get a builder anything he wants, even from a picture in a magazine."

Olden, who still works with some multifamily clients, must do a different kind of sourcing for them, especially companies such as Beacon Construction Co. in Newport News, which specializes in affordable multifamily housing. The niche demands that Olden stay on top of material prices and new technology to keep costs in check. "Over time, I've completely rewritten some of my clients specs," he says. I've become close enough to them and their architects that I can substitute products, if necessary.

"I try to give him as much of my business as possible," says George Mirmelstein, Beacons's vice president of construction. "Clint won't hesitate to warn me off a new

product if he thinks it won't stand up."

More than once, Olden has come through in a pinch. Mirmelstein recalls the time that Olden special ordered locksets with a distinctive finish for a job. The locksets looked too good: A few were stolen on the jobsite, leading to panic. "Clint had replacements sent to the job site the next day," he says.

Sawyer tries to stay close enough to each job to recognize potential code violations, particularly when he's on site measuring for stairs or a window that is supposed to provide fire egress. His code expertise is recognized by customers who ask for his help to get blueprints through the city permit office. "There will be slight changes to the plan, and they will ask me to make sure the new specs will pass," he says.

Sawyer uses a computer to keep track of the options offered by his builder clients and changes during construction. "Tract houses now have pages and pages of options," he says. Some of them are major, like finishing bonus rooms; others involve different window configurations or door specs. But overlooking even one can foul up the builder's schedule. "Every variation is on the computer, so all we have to do is punch it up to create the right order," he says. "I'd be lost without it."

Technical knowledge is the foundation of these building products sales representatives' success. Without that knowledge they wouldn't sell very much.

Passing On Knowledge

Having technical knowledge is one matter. But passing on that knowledge to your customer or prospect in a way that propels the purchasing decision, may be another matter.

Early in my sales training, Gordon told a story to illustrate the value of correctly passing on knowledge. When polyethylene was a new plastic, someone in the DuPont Company conceived the idea of applying a thin coating of it on kraft paper. Because of the properties of the plastic, it seemed that polyethylene-coated paper could offer many possibilities in use.

Gordon was a member of the sales team involved in the introduction to the paper industry. He was armed with impressive data sheets listing the physical and chemical properties of the various densities of polyethylene. The initial response from the research directors who heard his presentation and saw the data was polite disinterest.

On the second tour of the paper companies, Gordon had the same data sheets, but this time also had small molded rectangular pieces made of different polyethylene densities. The paper company research people felt the pieces, flexed them, and calmly speculated on what uses might be found for paper coated with one of these plastics. But beyond this mild interest, paper companies gave no commitments for action.

At about this time, one of the DuPont engineers constructed a laboratory-size extruder to coat a six-inch web of paper. At the next gathering of the sales team, he demonstrated this extruder and gave each sales rep a few feet of the polyethylene-coated kraft paper.

One member of the sales force did one more thing. He took the coated paper home, cut a twelve-inch length and folded it in half with the plastic coating on the inside. With a hot iron, he sealed two sides forming an open-ended pouch. He then poured water into the open end and sealed the last side. In doing so, he formed a paper bag of water, completely enclosed. The plastic was not visible; it appeared as though by some magic, water was contained by kraft paper (which anybody who has suffered a wet grocery bag knows is impossible).

Polyethylene is water impermeable. Paper companies at that time produced water-resistant papers, but none that could literally hold water. Each member of the sales force instantly recognized the potential drama of showing kraft paper pouches of water and rushed home to make their own pouches.

As expected, the display of the paper pouch of water on the next tour of the paper companies proved electrifying. Gordon vividly remembered walking into the office of one research director with whom he had discussed polyethylene use on two previous trips. Without saying anything else, Gordon almost shouted, "Did you ever see a paper bag full of water?" as he tossed the pouch on the director's desk.

The director leaped to his feet, grabbed the pouch, and rushed out of the office. After about ten minutes, he came back. "Come with me! Our president wants to see you!" These words were spoken by a very excited man. This was the same director of research who had glanced at the data sheets on the first visit and had handled the molded plastic rectangles with little interest on the second visit.

The chemical and physical properties of the polyethylene were clearly defined on the data sheets. Any scientist with the background of this paper company research director could easily look at the data and visualize the water impermeability, the flexibility at various temperatures, the toughness, and many other useful properties.

Or, if he couldn't visualize the end-use opportunities

from the figures and graphs, you would think that holding, feeling, flexing, hammering, and tearing the molded pieces of plastic he handled on the second visit should have been more than enough to excite his interest. One would have thought the potential value of this new development was clear. But that wasn't enough. It wasn't enough for him nor was it enough for any of the other paper company research directors.

Demonstration, specific demonstration of what the product could do in an end-use application, was the key. Seeing and feeling the coated paper and the paper bag of water bridged the canyon, and did it quickly. Maybe over a long period of time, some of these same scientists would have arrived at the same conclusion, the same result. But, not so soon. Dramatic demonstration achieved a result that had defied conventional approach.

The effect at all paper companies was similar, if not always as explosive. Commitments for the immediate installation of extruders followed and the polyethylene coating of paper was launched.

The product and concept Gordon tried to sell on the first visit were identical to the product and concept presented on the third visit. The only difference was demonstration.

Demonstration as a selling tool is employed often, and sometimes in a highly sophisticated manner. Advertising agencies, for example, prepare a proposed ad campaign for a prospective client in order to get that client's business. Most automobile salespeople will invite you to drive a new car like the one you are considering. Some furniture retailers will encourage you to put the new furniture in your home and see how you like it. If you are not satisfied with it, they'll come pick it up.

There are, however, many overlooked opportunities for demonstration. There are many things an individual salesperson can do which depend on nothing more than a little imagination. You demonstrate a feature to buyers in order to dramatize a benefit.

If it is sharp, let them cut something with it. If it is tough, hand them hammers and let them pound on it. If it is soft, let them feel it. If it will help something grow, show them.

If you can swing it, paint it, bounce it, throw it, drop it, or kick it, let the customer swing it, paint it, throw it, drop it, or kick it.

If you have competition, and if the buyer's choice will be made largely on a comparison of your products and the competitive products, then demonstrate both yours and the competitive products. Wouldn't you prefer to demonstrate how your product performs against the competitor's rather than the competitor demonstrate their product against yours?

If you are selling tractors, why not have a complete file of competitors' literature ready to show the customer? Even better than that, park your tractor right between those of your two leading competitors in your back showroom or on your lot. "You'd like to compare, sir? Please come with me. We can do it right here and now."

Successful sellers demonstrate. If you are not demonstrating, think about how you could. If you are demonstrating, think about how you could do it better -- do it with more impact.

If a method of demonstration for your product or service is not readily apparent, ask a few potential buyers, "What could I do to demonstrate to you the value of this product?" Then, if the answer is within reason, do it -- for this buyer and for the others who are purchasing for a similar use.

Words and literature are seldom enough. "Seeing is believing." Let your buyers "see" for themselves. Demonstrate. You will write more orders and create more customers if you do.

Nothing Rates Higher Than Technical Knowledge

I use the word "technical" in the sense of concern with the technicalities or minute points of a product or situation. You must know it all to be an effective seller.

First, you should have an intimate knowledge of your own products, what they will do and, as importantly, what they will not do. Second, you must know the competitive products and their strengths and weaknesses. Third, you must know your customers' business in order to match your features in ways beneficial to their needs and wants.

I'd be willing to wager that more than fifty percent of all winning salespeople's success derives from their technical knowledge. In the particular case of Harold it may have been closer to one hundred percent.

If you are getting along in selling without a depth of knowledge, as many are, I am confident you can increase your successes and your income by learning more. When you become an admired source of knowledge about your products and their applications, your competitors' products and your markets, you will be proud of your accomplishments. You also will earn more money.

Without equivocation, of all the qualities that go into successful salesmanship, technical knowledge stands out as one with major importance.

Have More Fun

This book plays on a valuable axiom. It may be more apparent in this area of technical knowledge than in others.

The axiom is this: The better you do something the more fun and satisfaction there is in doing it.

The golfer who wins the Masters at Augusta, Georgia, has more fun, greater satisfaction and warmer memories than the person who places second and more, for sure, than those who didn't even make the cut.

Baseball players who consistently bat above .300 have more fun than those who struggle to reach .200. Ask them -- but you don't even have to do that. Just look at them as they either streak toward first base or walk back to the dugout, heads hung down and shoulders slumped.

Look at the face of the professional tennis player as she accepts the first-place trophy for a tennis tournament and compare it to the face of the woman standing beside her, defeated. Which one is having more fun, which one enjoys the greatest satisfaction?

Sports stars reach the top because of a certain amount of natural talent. However, when you dig into their background, their formative years and their daily routine while they are at the top, you find without exception: hard work and unrelenting practice.

The same holds true in selling. The more knowledge you stow away about your product, the more hands-on experience you have with it, the more fun you will have selling it. It is fun to be an expert. It is fun to know there is no question you cannot answer in detail. It is fun to have others look up to you and say, "Please teach me."

Acquire all the technical knowledge you can and continue to acquire it as long as you're selling. It is not only an attribute that will contribute materially to your success, but also a source of deep, personal satisfaction.

There Are Exceptions

Maybe the product you sell is not technical in nature. Some products are so simple in composition and use there is really no technical information to learn. If such is your case, rejoice. There are only four attributes for you to acquire. Jump on the next one -- you'll like it. Everyone deals with people.

CHAPTER 2

SINCERE INTEREST IN PEOPLE

"I have never had four walls, a roof or a factory give me business. Only people can sign orders."
Arnold L. Schwartz, **Dynamic Professional Selling,**
Nichols Publishing
New York, NY

Summary: A sincere interest in people will increase your sales.

One of the most skillful face-to-face salespersons I ever knew possessed a large fund of knowledge about the people with whom he dealt. On a sales call, everyone, not only the buyer, treated him like a welcomed friend.

It wasn't difficult to see why they greeted Russ so cordially. From the reception desk all the way back to the buyer's corner office, Russ called each person by name. He had either a word for them or a smile.

"One Fine Fellow"

On more than one occasion I observed Russ make deft use of personal information he had gathered about a person. However, the first time I was consciously aware of what he was doing was a day we were having lunch with one of his customers. During a lull in the conversation, Russ turned to the customer and said, "Bill, how is your oldest boy doing at Ohio State? This is his third year, isn't it?"

You could see a warm glow spread over Bill's face as he replied, "He's doing just great. How did you know? Yes, this is his third year and if it's like the first two I couldn't be happier – in fact he made the Dean's list both years."

I couldn't help noticing both surprise and pleasure on Bill's face. From the way he said, "How did you know?" I gathered he didn't remember having talked to Russ about his son. There was no doubt he was happy the subject came up. Bragging about the accomplishments of a son or daughter even beats bragging about a hole-in-one.

What did Russ get out of it? He got unspoken gratitude for having made Bill feel good. Six months later Bill couldn't have told you why he feels about Russ the way he does. However, Bill did say to me some months later when we met at a convention, "That Russ is one fine fellow."

Put on the buyer's shoes for a moment.

Is it easier to do business with "one fine fellow" than with someone you have no particular feelings about? Are you likely to give a little more business to "one fine fellow" than you are to a person you can take or leave? Obvious answers!

Yet, it is peculiar that few salespeople make any attempt to develop a file of personal information about their customers or even make use of the morsels gratuitously dropped in their laps.

Remembering

Getting back to the incident between Russ and Bill -- after we dropped Bill back at his office and started down the road toward the next call, I asked Russ how he knew Bill's oldest son was studying at Ohio State.

"He told me, but he's forgotten -- it was three years ago. One day when I was in to see him, Bill casually mentioned he was going to high school graduation that night. I asked him who was graduating and he told me it was his oldest son. Then, I asked the obvious next question about what he would be doing after graduation. He answered `He'll enter Ohio State this fall' and we dropped the subject."

Somehow, Russ' answer didn't completely satisfy me. I decided to probe a little deeper.

"How many active accounts do you have, Russ?"

"Oh, I don't know -- about a hundred I guess."

"And," I continued, "how many people do you deal with in each of those one hundred accounts?"

"Three, maybe four," he replied.

"Ok, let's say it averages three-and-one-half. Multiplied by one hundred, that is three hundred fifty people you have to get to know; three hundred fifty individuals, each with his or her own background, family, personality and interests. Bill is just one out of three hundred fifty. How could you possibly remember that it was Bill and not Tom, Elaine, or Mike who told you three years ago that their oldest son was entering Ohio State?"

"I see what you're driving at," Russ said. "The answer is simple. I didn't remember it. I don't even try. I write down personal information as I pick it up."

"Here," as he pulled a card from his inside coat pocket,

"is a 3" x 5" index card I call my People Card. This is the one for Bill's company. I pulled it out of the file last night when I was preparing for these calls today. I simply refreshed my memory about personal things Bill has mentioned."

Russ wrote his card in long-hand using a pencil so he could erase information as it became outdated. Here is the kind of information he recorded:

> **NAME:** Johnson Machine Products Co.
>
> **ADDRESS:** 17 Second St., Anytown, USA
>
> **Phone:** 555 555 5555
>
> **NAME:** William S. Johnson (Bill) **TITLE:** Pres.
>
> **BD:** 7/18 **I-H-N:** Avid Chicago Bears fan. Golfer.
>
> Occasional fishing. Home woodworking shop.
>
> BS Engineer U of Ill.
>
> **WIFE:** Mildred **WA:** 10/25
>
> SS Teacher. Good bridge player.
>
> **CHILDREN:**
>
> Wm. S. Jr. '68 Enter Ohio State 9/86-Bus. Adm.
>
> Marsha '72; John '75

"Well, just off hand," I commented, "this looks simple enough. I assume 'BD' means birthday. Why didn't you write down the year as well as the day and month?"

"Because, I don't know the year. Some people are proud of their age and some others would prefer you not know. If the customer doesn't drop the information in conversation, I don't make a special effort to find out. As a matter a fact, Bill didn't tell me the date of his birthday, his secretary mentioned it one day. Even if a person doesn't want his age known, it pleases all the people I know to have somebody say, `Happy Birthday' either with a card, a phone call or in person. I use all three depending on the circumstances."

"What does `I-H-N' stand for?" I asked.

"That is just shorthand for Interest-Hobbies-Notes. Actually, I don't need the label because what I write there is obvious. I've dropped the label, but not the information, from my new cards and gained a little space.

"You pick up clues about your customers just by looking around their offices -- plaques showing awards, clubs they belong to, schools they attended. Do they have splendid or spartan furnishings? Is their desk clean or piled with paper? People provide road signs about themselves in many ways other than words," Russ explained.

"If you'll turn over that card you'll see I have two other people in Bill's company written up on the back side. If I need more space, which is seldom the case, I staple a second card to the first."

"I notice you have Bill's wife's name but you don't show her birthday. Why is that? And what does `WA' stand for?"

"WA stands for Wedding Anniversary. I wouldn't make any effort to get that date, but in Bill's case, he, his wife and I were out for dinner one night and they made a point of telling me the next night was their wedding anniversary. I thought if it was important enough to them to bring it up, it might be a good idea to note the date and send a card each year.

"That is what I've done and Bill never fails to mention that his wife really appreciates the anniversary card. I have never figured out why wedding anniversaries seem more important to wives than to husbands.

"And you're right, I don't have a record of Bill's wife's birthday. It has never come up and it probably won't. Whether or not I'd record the date I can't say. It would depend on the circumstances."

Don't Conduct A Quiz

"That leads me to emphasize something," Russ went on. "The personal information you get from a customer has to come naturally. You can't conduct a quiz to fill out your card. That would defeat the whole idea. If I have never met a customer's wife, I don't care when her birthday is or their wedding anniversary. If I have met her and if she has mentioned the dates, I might send a greeting or I might not. It depends.

"On the other hand, I know salespeople who don't write down anything. About the third time in two years the customer has to say `I have a wife and three children' he is ready to throw up because he realizes the sales representative is simply feigning interest when asking, `How many children do you have?' That salesperson has hurt himself. It would be better to keep the conversation focused entirely on business topics and away from personal areas.

"If the personal side of people doesn't genuinely interest you, being artificial will show and that is not attractive. In that case, stay away from personal talk, or find another job that is less people-important."

Respond To Friendship

"I've noticed a curious fact," Russ continued. "It is this: People more clearly remember what they tell other people than those people remember what they were told. If I tell you that I went to the University of Florida for four years and earned a degree in civil engineering, I am more likely to remember that I told you than you are to remember what I said.

"That is another reason for recording personal data as you pick it up. If I think enough of you to tell you personal things and if you do not think enough of me to remember, you are rebuffing me. I'm going to be annoyed -- maybe not a lot and to be sure not openly, but I will resent it a little and it will tarnish our relationship. Contrast that to the warmth you could create by adroit use of personal facts as you saw with Bill at lunch today."

"That brings up a point I wanted to ask you. Have you never mentioned his son attending Ohio State in the three years since he first told you?"

"No," Russ said. "As a matter of fact I don't think I have. It is not that I purposely avoided it, but rather there was never an occasion when a question or comment about it seemed appropriate -- never a time when it would have fit unobtrusively into the conversation. You must do it with finesse or don't do it at all."

Recap Information

"I'll tell you what else I do with these people cards," Russ volunteered. "I recap some of the information to make it more useful."

"What do you mean?"

"Well, take birthdays, for example. I keep a database of all birthdays on my computer -- my family, my wife's family, friends and customers. It is in chronological order. That makes it easy to send cards or telephone or see them at the right time.

"I also maintain a special interest database. I've got lists on travel, football, baseball, fishing, golf, tennis, bridge, and even one on gourmet cooking.

"These lists have come in handy several times to get people , together with common interests or to invite customers to a sporting event. Occasionally, my wife makes a short trip with me. We both play bridge and have had several enjoyable evenings with a bridge-playing customer and his or her spouse. Knowing your customer's spouse and having them know yours adds substantially to a smooth-working relationship.

"These special-interest lists also give me an opportunity to clip articles out of a newspaper or magazine and drop them in the mail to those who care about a particular subject. It always results in a favorable comment, sometimes even a note in return."

The Edge

Russ continued, "One day I was telling another salesperson about my people cards and he said, `But, that is artificial. People don't genuinely interest you or you wouldn't be writing down what they tell you and then checking your notes just before calling on them again.'

"I was probably shouting when I responded with, `Look you idiot, I record personal data solely because I can't remember everything. The fact that I write it down and keep it clearly shows that people interest me more than they do you. When I see customers I want to talk about the subjects they want to talk about and avoid those that irritate. Some of my cards have notes like, `stay away from politics' or `hates baseball.' If my customer is divorced, I don't want to ask `How is your wife?' or `How is your husband?'

"`There is nothing artificial about my people cards. I do have a genuine interest in people. You are the one who does not. You won't make the small effort to write down these personal facts on their behalf, not to mention for your own benefit.'

"Here in my mind is what the it boils down to," Russ concluded, "selling is a personal affair. You are more likely to buy from a person you like than one you're indifferent to. I'm hoping my customers will like me a little more than they like my competitor because they interest me as individuals, not solely as buyers. It is not a big deal, but I think it helps a little and in most negotiations a small edge is all I need."

What can I add? Russ said it all. Selling *is* a personal affair. It sure is. And I suspect Russ' edge was bigger than he thought it was.

Two Characteristics

In a workshop for sales managers one day, I asked, "If you could have only two characteristics in a sales representative, what would they be?"

The participants had no time to ponder the question before expressing their response. These were the first words out of t..._r mouths and, in every case, without hesitation:

- Great listener and willing to work
- Enthusiasm and strong commitment
- Ability to communicate and motivated
- Prior selling success and high moral value
- Greed and willingness to work
- Integrity and communication skills
- Positive attitude and product knowledge
- Likable and bright

Identifying only two characteristics was a tough order. This list of eight pairs contains thirteen different characteristics -- I'd like to have all of them. Admittedly, some of them you might not classify as characteristics, but that is not important. This was not an exercise in semantics.

The group took issue with the person who said "greed". He explained that he was talking about a strong desire to earn a lot of money. Others tried to guide him toward a word less harsh, but he wouldn't budge. So greed it was.

The sales manager who said "likable and bright" went on to explain that the choice was not original with him. He knew a sales manager who had an enviable record not only for high sales volume, but also for very low sales force turnover.

Someone asked that successful manager to describe his interviewing techniques. His answer was this:

"I spend a lot of time with the candidate. We'll go to a sporting event -- maybe a baseball game -- we'll have dinner together, or anything else the candidate would like to do. The interview could take more than one day. At the end of that time, if I like the candidate, I know our customers will too.

"People try to avoid buying from a person they don't like. On the other hand, they'll go out of their way to buy from someone they do like."

The manager went on to say, "My second characteristic should be obvious. You can't teach product knowledge and price lists to a dummy. I need bright people for our sales force. You can tell a lot about a person's brains through conversation over a range of subjects, including current events. If I think I need more evidence, I can look at their college transcript. Of course, the candidate may not have one -- all bright people do not go to college.

"Anyway, the results satisfy me. I've gotten what I need looking for just those two characteristics -- likable and bright."

In that workshop, the participants turned the tables and asked for my response to the same question. Turnabout is fair play, so here was my answer:

Caring and curious.

Caring people will be sensitive to the wants, needs, and the moods of other people. They will cheer with them in times of joy, and weep with them in times of grief. Customers will love them, not because of dramatic actions, but on the contrary, because of quiet, steady devotion to the monetary and emotional welfare of the customer over a long period.

In his book, *Notes From A Briefcase*, Steve Stevenson wrote this:

"Smart salespeople take the time to remember by mail. They know a thank you or a congratulatory note is always read and appreciated, although the recipient may not mention it.

"For instance, I once received a note from a sales rep

who had contacted me concerning a project in which I felt I had no interest. The note read, in part, `Yesterday you gave me a gift of a part of your time. It was a gift only you could give. Thank you.' I decided I might be interested in the project after all. The note was sincere because the sales rep was that kind of person."

That was a caring salesperson.

Caring people are selfless. They think more of others than of themselves. How you feel this morning concerns them more than how they feel. They want to talk about you. They want you to talk about yourself. Indeed, you will tell caring people more than you realize while they tell you little about themselves.

Gordon told me about a salesman he once knew. Jess had much in his background and life he could have talked about. His father was a renowned professor at Columbia University in New York City. He also was the editor of a prestigious journal and a highly paid industry consultant. Jess' sister was an editor for *Reader's Digest* -- an enviable position for a journalist.

Jess, himself, had graduated from Columbia at age seventeen with a chemistry degree. After Columbia, farming attracted him. He went to Maryland, got a job on a dairy farm and married the farmer's daughter when they were both eighteen. They had ten children. Jess also attended the University of Maryland and earned another degree -- this one in agriculture.

Gordon knew all of this because he and Jess traveled together for nine years and they talked a lot. Gordon also met Jess' wife and their ten children.

Jess left the company and moved on to other work. Over the following years Gordon talked to many of Jess' customers. The subject of Jess always came up, usually at the outset. They all wanted to know where he was and what he was doing. They all regretted his departure and had complimentary remarks about him. Even after ten years had passed, some of them were still asking.

Yet not one of these customers knew much about Jess. They didn't know he had ten children. They didn't know he graduated from college at age seventeen and was married at eighteen. They hadn't heard of his father and sister.

Gordon told me he never heard one derogatory reference to Jess. All his customers thought he was a wonderful person and, yet, they knew little about him.

Jess didn't go out of his way to avoid talking about himself. That wasn't the reason his customers knew little about him. The reason was that people like to talk about themselves. Jess knew that and exploited it to his advantage. People liked Jess because he allowed them to talk about themselves. He listened and what they said genuinely interested him.

You Can Learn

If you do not have a natural bent toward caring, can you learn to be caring? Yes, you can. You can learn to do anything if you really want to.

Start with a piece of paper and a pencil. Make a list of the background items, accomplishments and activities of your life you would enjoy telling other people -- things you would like to tell social acquaintances or customers. Opposite each item write the questions a person could ask you to get you to talk about that item.

The items in the first column are close to the what others would like to tell you about themselves. In the second column, you now have a list of questions you can pose to people that will get them to talk about themselves.

Here's a tip about something I've used many times. It is particularly effective with the owner of a business.

After you've known people long enough to feel comfortable with them -- say after two or three calls -- and you are in a semi-social, relaxed atmosphere, such as over the breakfast or lunch table, calmly ask, "How did you get started in this business?"

The floodgates open. You'd better have some time to spend. ·The flow will continue as you respond with an occasional, "Really?" or "Why that?" interspersed with some timely "Uh-huh"s.

Forget about yourself. People want to talk about one thing -- about themselves. Selling is a people business. If you want to be successful in a people business, you have to make it easy for people to talk about themselves. Plant that firmly in your mind.

Furthermore, there is delightful serendipity. While accomplishing your goal of strengthening rapport, you'll hear some fascinating stories. You win twice.

Some Don't Talk

It is absolutely true, most people like to talk about themselves. However, don't overlook the word "most." It means some do not. Some people are very private -- they purposely avoid talking about themselves and their interests. You won't see a family picture on their desk.

Don't intrude on a person's privacy. If your customers don't talk about themselves, it's because they don't want to. Treat them the way they want you to treat them.

How will you know if the prospect you just met prefers privacy or an open relationship? You won't know right away because even those who like to talk don't usually open up to strangers. The information you collect about a person develops over time as your relationship matures. It does not tumble forth at the outset nor as the result of questioning. Avoid direct questioning -- it can easily slip into being obtrusive and that leads to obnoxious.

The personal information you collect, and later use advantageously as Russ did, develops from conversations over meals more than from talk across the desk. Nevertheless, be alert to pick up interesting facts anytime, anywhere. You can't predict when they will fall.

If your customers seem to maintain a wall of privacy, if they stiffen when you get on the fringes of personal matters, back off. You can lose if you try to become close with a person who resents closeness with vendors.

Some people don't even let those within their own company get close to them. Crawford Greenewalt, a former chairman of DuPont, wrote that he had never met the wives of most of the senior officers of his company and didn't care to. Business life was one thing and social life something else. He didn't want to mix the two.

The most prosperous salespeople adjust to their customers. They are excellent readers of their customers' likes and dislikes. They know if they should indulge in small talk or get right to business. They know if their customers have a sense of humor or not. They know if their customers need to be led to make a decision or pride themselves in assembling all the facts and making their own decisions.

The best sales representatives change themselves as they move from customer to customer. They always present the kind of person they know the customer wants to see. They are skillful actors.

Yes, most people like to talk about themselves and, if you can't remember the other part, you'll be in the right groove ninety percent of the time. However, if you want to make it one hundred percent, keep in mind there are some who don't want to talk about personal matters. If you let your customers and prospects be the kind of person they want to be, you'll be the winning salesperson.

Dress

"Personal appearance may not be important, but it may reflect the neatness of one's mind."
      Frank Petrini, 1900-1994

A sincere interest in people, and in your own success, includes thinking about the visual image you present to customers and prospects.

How does one dress? How should a salesperson dress when calling on customers? I don't know the answer. I don't know, that is, in specific terms such as a "gray suit and striped tie" or such as "always a skirt and never pants."

Times change; tastes change; places change. And, there are the obvious considerations of, "What is the occasion? What is the weather? What is the time of day?" It is possible, however, to outline some general considerations that you can apply to specific situations provided the person applying them is observant and has some taste.

You can begin by asking yourself, "How do I want to feel?" Clothes do affect your feelings. It is virtually undeniable that putting on a new, clean, well-designed garment has a salutary influence on ones feelings. Does it not make you stand a bit taller, force your shoulders back, give you a more confident step and a firmer handshake?

A good friend of mine, Kelly, is a highly successful entrepreneur. His human resources consulting business is located in an impressive suite of offices. When Kelly started his business fifteen years ago, his office was in the attic of his house. He was the only employee. No one saw Kelly in the course of the business day except his wife when he came to the kitchen for lunch. Each day however, Kelly dressed as if he were going to an office on Wall Street. A clean, crisply starched white shirt, dark suit, conservative tie, and highly polished shoes constituted his "uniform of the day". Why? He felt more professional and he believed that feeling translated over the telephone as he called on prospects to establish a customer base. I think he was right.

Wearing clothes is not unlike wearing facial expressions. It is generally conceded that a smile on your face reflects a happy feeling inside just as a frown reflects an inner worry or uncertainty. But it is less widely recognized that you can change your inner feelings by forcing a change in your outer expressions. For example, if you force a smile on your face it is impossible to remain unhappy inside.

We have all heard allusions, in various ways, to the benefits of singing while you work. It is the same principle. Singing normally results from a feeling of happiness. Conversely, making yourself sing, just as with smiling, can induce a feeling of happiness. Therefore, if you sing while you work you are happier, the work becomes lighter and more bearable and you are the beneficiary.

Knowing you are well dressed gives you confidence, self-assurance, and an overall feeling of well-being.

Knowing you are poorly dressed does just the opposite. "I sure hope I don't run into so-and-so dressed the way I am" is not an uncommon thing to say to yourself.

So, dress for the way you want to feel.

A second consideration is to dress in conformity with the image you want to project to the customer. How do you want the customer to perceive you? After all, impressions are formed about people based on their clothes. If a person is dressed in dirty, rumpled work clothes· you get one impression. If you see red plaid trousers or skirt and a bright orange sweater you get another impression. Or, if you see a person in a clean, pressed, well-tailored, color-coordinated outfit, you get still a third impression.

If you want to project the image of a careless, disorganized, and self-centered sales representative then you will dress in loose, unpressed casual clothes of any color or type combination that happens to be handy to wear. You really don't care how you look.

On the other hand if you wish the customer to perceive you as a professional business person, more concerned with him or her than with yourself, more interested in pleasing than in being pleased, you will dress conservatively, unostentatiously, in a style that reflects a neat, organized, successful, tasteful business person. Your clothes will reflect an attitude which says, "I think enough of you to take the trouble to dress up for you, not to show off but to show respect."

A third consideration in picking your mode of dress is to meet the customer's expectation or, to put it in a slightly different way, to dress so that the customer feels comfortable in your presence. Dressing so the customer feels comfortable in your presence may mean that you wear clothing similar to what the customer is wearing. If the customer dresses casually, you dress casually. If he or she wears formal business garments, then you wear formal business garments. That is one possible approach to take but it is not necessarily the only one.

If the buyers customarily wear casual attire in their places of business it does not necessarily follow that they expect you to wear similar clothing nor that they are most comfortable with you when you do. They may expect you to wear more formal business clothes, something that would more nearly correspond to their image of your role.

For example, you decide to purchase credit from a bank and the banker meets you in faded blue jeans and a turtleneck sweater. It would probably take that banker some period of time to establish his or her position, reliability, and reason for deserving your business; certainly longer than if the clothing conformed to the more traditional banker attire.

Or, to look at the other extreme, suppose you called a plumber to come to your house and he showed up dressed in a clean shirt and designer tie, a well-pressed, expensive business suit, highly polished shoes, and manicured fingernails. This certainly wouldn't fit your expectation and you would be thrown off balance. Wouldn't it take some time to convince you that he is a capable plumber before you would let him put a wrench on your pipes?

So, dressing to match your customer's attire is the correct answer only part of the time. Maybe a better answer is this: to be dressed in such a way that five minutes after you are gone, if somebody asked the person you visited how you were dressed, he or she would be incapable of giving a detailed description.

That is a good answer. And yet there are exceptions to

that concept.

Some sales representatives are engaged in selling products or services that can be obtained in identical form from a number of different suppliers at comparable prices. The major thing these sellers have to sell is *themselves*. A technique sometimes employed is to create some distinction -- to do things, wear things or to employ accouterments that stand out and receive favorable comments from customers. The most common example is an article of clothing or an entire outfit, perhaps expensive, always in good taste, and yet distinctive enough that it receives attention and is admired.

A cane or walking stick, an unusual briefcase, or a unique calling card could serve the same purpose and be even more noticeable. I once knew a salesman, Guy, who was an extremely successful seller of a very common commodity. Guy had a dog, a Boxer, which he had trained to perfection. Everywhere he went the dog was at his heels; its obedience was flawless. The dog went along on every customer call and became a welcomed and looked-forward-to visitor in every buyer's office. The Boxer was Guy's trademark -- it made him agreeably distinctive.

A few years ago I was close to the owner of a small manufacturing firm who was also his own salesman. The product he manufactured could be purchased from a dozen similar companies. Success led him to want a luxury car. But, he was concerned that his customers, when they saw the car, would think he didn't need their business, would give orders to his competitors and he would end up with less business.

He worried for three years about whether to purchase the car. However, one day he decided business was so good he could afford to take the chance. So, he purchased the luxury car and began to use it for his business calls. He couldn't believe the results.

Contrary to his worries, buyers who had been cool to him were now anxious to go out to lunch to ride in his new luxury car. His business grew even more rapidly and he told me his only regret was that he had not made the plunge earlier. The car became his trademark -- buyers were pleased to be seen in the company of a person so obviously successful.

What, then, is the bottom line? Where do we end up on this question of dress? We talked about your own feelings, the image you want to project, and the image the customer expects. Here are three guidelines about dress:

1. Buy high quality clothes and footwear. Pay fifty percent to one hundred percent more than you've been used to paying. One high quality garment will outlast two or three cheap ones. It will hold its form, it will clean and press well, and you will feel well dressed in it for a very long time.

2. Coordinate colors. Buy accessories -- scarves, ties, blouses, shirts -- that complement the principle clothing.

3. Dress at least a little better than your customers. They want to deal with successful sellers. They want to look up to you. The buyer wants to be proud to introduce you to the president if your paths should cross. Your manner, your general demeanor will illustrate that you are not dressing to show off. Rather, you are dressing to show respect for your customer and to gain respect for yourself.

It is commonly said that people are known by the company they keep. It is just as true that they are known by the clothes they wear. As a sales representative you want to be known in a way that will most enhance the possibility of getting an order.

Physical Barriers

You wouldn't try to talk with the buyer on the other side of a wall or with you and the buyer so far apart you can't hear each other. Of course, you wouldn't.

However, more subtle barriers can exist. If you recognize them, and take appropriate action, you can enhance your chances of success as well as display your sincere interest in your prospect or customer.

The absence of physical barriers to verbal, visual and emotional communications will promote understanding and acceptance. Breaking down the barriers may not assure success in an individual case but will raise the success average -- over a period of time or over a number of cases.

The first, and perhaps most common barrier is the desk. The buyer sits behind a desk which gives a sense of security, a defense against the seller on the opposite side of the desk.

The desk does not have to be an actual desk. A table, a counter top or any piece of furniture will do. The wider it is the better -- better, that is, for a defensive purpose. In most cases it is unlikely the buyer consciously thinks of the desk as a physical defensive barrier and, indeed, it may not be. Business is often successfully negotiated across a desk. Nevertheless, a desk *is* a physical barrier and can be put to defensive use if the buyer wishes to do so.

Why is a desk a physical barrier? It is for several reasons. It undeniably puts a certain distance between the buyer and the seller and the wider the desk the greater the distance. Distance does not promote warmth and friendliness between people. It is easier to reject someone at a distance than it is when you are close to them. It is easier to say "No" to a salesperson across a desk than it is when standing face to face or when sitting side by side.

The main reason for taking buyers to lunch is to get them out from behind their desks and closer to you. As you walk down the street side by side there is a greater feeling of camaraderie. You choose a table in the restaurant so you can sit at right angles to one another. If an order is still hanging in the balance, you get agreement while you are next to each other at the table. It is the most favorable place. If you wait until you return to the office where the buyer again gets behind the barrier, the desk, you will reduce your order percentage because he or she can more easily say, "No."

Let's reverse the situation for just a minute. Imagine that you, the seller, were in your office seated at your desk. A buyer comes to see you. You begin to talk about your product or service. Do you really believe you would stay behind that desk? Of course not. As you warmed to your subject and as your enthusiasm grew, would you not come out from behind your desk and move closer to the buyer? It would be a most natural move to make.

Think about the public speakers you have heard. There are two kinds: those who lean on the podium and those who leave the podium. Which speakers are the most effective? Is it those who stand behind the podium, never leaving it, or is it those who walk away from the podium and stand before you at full height with no barrier, no podium, nothing between them and the audience? Which speakers seem to speak more directly to you? Which speakers seem more interesting and more sincere? Which speakers more successfully convey their messages?

Admittedly, you must vary your technique to suit each individual buyer. There are those who might be repulsed if you tried to get too close -- they value their distance. If you are getting all the orders you want across the desk, stay with it. But if you are not getting enough business, at least consider the possibility that removing the desk barrier might help. There are cases where it will.

The second physical impediment to communicating effectively and nurturing smooth, warm, understanding buyer-seller relations, is eye glasses.

"Eye glasses? Oh c'mon," you say, "I need my glasses. You're not going to tell me not to wear them, are you?"

No, but we can look at some things to consider when wearing glasses -- things which some salespeople don't think about.

Eyes are perhaps the most expressive part of a person's face. Without moving any part of our body nor, indeed, any other part of the face it is possible, through the eyes alone, to express a complete range of emotions from joy to anger. Songs are written about love expressed through the eyes. When you talk to another person in either a business or a social situation, you are constantly reading their eyes both when they are talking and when you are talking.

If we have agreement to this point it should not be difficult to move to the next point: the buyer has a need to read the eyes of the seller. (Indeed, the reciprocal of that statement is equally true, but a sales representative cannot say to a buyer, "Please take off your glasses.")

The buyer needs to read the sales representative's eyes

to add to the words being heard. He or she can read emotion through the eyes and compute the degree of correlation with the spoken word. If there is little correlation the buyer's mental computer will give a signal to hold off, to press for more information, or to reject the proposal. If there is a high degree of correlation it reinforces the buyer's confidence in his or her ultimate judgment as the order is signed.

Unfortunately there is not a broad recognition of this principle among sellers. Sales representatives do not willfully violate the principle we are discussing, they just don't *think* about it. So, let's think about it.

Do you ever wear sunglasses while you're selling in an office environment? Of course not. You take off your sunglasses when you enter a building. But what about when you are selling outdoors on a bright, sunny day?

I'm not suggesting you strain your eyes in the sun. If you must, you can keep your glasses on during most of the conversation. But when you are approaching the moment where you will ask for commitment to the next step, take off your sunglasses and let the buyers see the enthusiasm, honesty, and sincerity reflected in your eyes. The emotion conveyed through your eyes is just as important as the words spoken through your lips.

Lenses which respond to varying degrees of light intensity have become popular. They darken in sunlight and become relatively clear in the absence of bright illumination such as in a building. However, they are never completely clear and obscure the eyes of the wearer more than clear lenses. To the degree they shade the eyes, they are a barrier to the viewer, the person to whom the wearer is talking, and ought not be worn when talking to a buyer.

The most common lenses, of course, are clear glass or

plastic. To the person looking at the wearer of such glasses, they afford a reasonably good view of the eyes except in those circumstances where there is a reflection on the lens. Then the eyes may be completely obscured without the wearer being cognizant of it. In this situation, the glasses hide the eyes. As the reflection dances about, it can become a significant distraction. Not only does the buyer fail to get eye messages, the distraction of the changing reflections prevents him from totally concentrating on the salesperson's words. Furthermore, the wearer of the glasses is totally unaware of the distracting reflection. You can avoid this phenomenon by spending a little more money for a lens coating that removes reflection.

Even under the best of circumstances with reflection-free lenses, glasses are a barrier. Eyes are more visible without them. There is greater opportunity for more intimate visual contact. If a sales representative facing a buyer wants to appear convincing, sincere, and dedicated, he should remove his glasses. If he doesn't take them off at the beginning, he should, at least, take off his glasses when he is preparing to ask for the commitment toward the next step.

I have seen professional sales representatives deploy their glasses with dramatic effect and dynamic results. In a case where the seller truly needs glasses to see and normally wears them all the time, as he or she draws to the end of the selling negotiations and is ready for the final statement and request for the order, the glasses are slowly and carefully removed. A move is made slightly closer to the buyer and the voice is perceptively lowered to a well modulated tone of sincerity as the sales representative looks the buyer directly in the eyes and says, "You have articulated your needs. We have demonstrated to your satisfaction that this product satisfies those needs by providing these benefits. Please give me the order now."

All barriers are down, this is toe to toe, eye to eye. No desk, no glasses. You will write more orders and create more customers if you'll remove the physical barriers. They are under your control.

Understand The Question

There is an old story about a mother and her eight-year-old son. One summer day Johnny came home from play and asked his mother, "Where did I come from?"

Johnny's mother knew that some day this question would come up. She had thought long about it and prepared for it. So she took Johnny by the hand, sat down on the sofa with him and explained all about mothers and fathers and babies in terms she thought he could understand.

When finally finished, she turned to her son and asked, "Now, Johnny, do you understand?"

"Well, not exactly, Mom," he said. "I was playing with Carl and he said he came from Cincinnati. I wondered where I came from."

The course of a conversation, or the circumstances of place and time, may make the meaning of a question clear. But there are many other instances where the intent of a question is obscure. To answer an obscure question without requesting clarification courts trouble.

Why should you ask for expansion of a question? Why should you seek better understanding? First of all it demonstrates respect for the person with whom you are talking. You show more than casual interest in the person and in what he or she wants to know. In some instances your conversational partner even expects you to request clarification and will be disappointed, if not displeased, when you do not.

If you do not grasp the true meaning of a question and yet attempt an answer, your interlocutor may think poorly of you. You depreciate yourself in his or her eyes. And in the case of a customer, that is very important to you.

The second reason you seek clarification of an obscure question, or a question with multiple possibilities, is that it is to your advantage to tell the customer only what he or she really wants to know. It can be to your disadvantage to get into areas that are not on the customer's mind or to expand your answer beyond what your buyer wants to know.

Let's take a simple, but not uncommon, example. Your plant is having temporary production problems and has put a two-week embargo on shipments. As you are writing the order, the customer asks, "When can you ship?" (The buyer is thinking, "I'd like to have it in thirty days.") You respond by saying, "We can't ship during the next two weeks, but there's no problem after that." There is a chance the customer will ask, "What is the problem in the next two weeks?"

At that point you wish you had kept your mouth shut. But, you are into it and have to explain the problem even though it jeopardizes the order. Wouldn't it have been wiser to respond to the first question with a qualifying question, "When do you want it?" The buyer would have responded, "In thirty days." You would have said, "Fine, it will be here," received a signed order and have been on your way.

People will sometimes pose questions where the intent is not evident to you nor to anybody else. Yet, the tendency of many of us is to make an assumption and give an answer without even a thought toward finding out what the person really wants to know.

Let's take an example. The buyer says to you, "Is this product tough?" You assume a tough product is wanted. So with great assurance you say, "Yes indeed, it is very tough." When the buyer retorts, "Well, then I can't use it," you sit back in amazement.

But, don't fault the buyer. The buyer wasn't trying to trap you. It was a legitimate question. The fault is yours for making an assumption. You failed to dig out the facts, to determine the buyer's needs and explore how your product might be used. In addition to that, "tough" is a relative term. One appropriate response might have been, "Tough compared to what?"

Sometimes the meaning of words escapes us. Yet for fear of appearing uneducated, we barge ahead without asking for the definition of the word we didn't know.

A few years ago, my wife and I attended a neighbor's cocktail party. The hostess and I were visiting and during our chat she asked, "What do you think of the new hirsute appendage?" and nodded toward the center of the room.

My mind went numb. Who wants to admit to his hostess, in whose home he is visiting for the first time, that she has a vocabulary beyond his level of comprehension?

So, glancing in the direction of her nod, I saw her husband talking to another guest and both were standing underneath a crystal chandelier that looked as though it could have been new and I instantly decided it was. "Hirsute" must be the designer or manufacturer's name like a Stiffel lamp or a Tiffany shade.

"It is beautiful. Very, very pretty. I've always admired chandeliers of that design," I said to her. She took a sip of her drink, smiled politely and turned to talk to another guest. There was no doubt I had blown it.

A little later, maneuvering my wife into a private corner, I whispered, "What is a hirsute appendage?"

"Hirsute has to do with hair," she said. "Why?"

"Well, our hostess asked me what I thought of the new hirsute appendage."

"Oh," she said, as a light came on, "She must have been referring to her husband's mustache. Now I know why he looks different than the last time I saw him. By the way, what did you say?"

And just then someone graciously broke into our conversation.

You wouldn't try to do business in a foreign language which you cannot speak. But, to a minor degree that is what you do if you let words or phrases get by you that you do not understand.

Unless your vocabulary is so limited that conversation is difficult and halting, no one is going to object to defining an occasional word and some will even be pleased you asked them.

The alternative of continuing to negotiate with a customer, not having understood a key word, can be disastrous. You ask, "But who would do a dumb thing like that?" Many people do. It happens every day.

It is not uncommon for a person to string together several questions without interruption. Usually only the last question or the next to the last question is answered, but the buyer doesn't know which of the several questions is drawing the response. Confusion is introduced, and confusion can benefit neither buyer nor seller.

If a customer asks several questions at once, separate them. Repeat the questions. Doing this will not only give you time to think, but also will permit you to see any association between questions. As you rephrase the questions, the customer will have an opportunity to insert corrections or amplifications if your repeated version is not precisely what the buyer meant to ask.

Finally, you can answer the questions one by one. This minimizes the chance for confusion or misunderstanding. And clear understanding is an essential ingredient in a sale and creating a satisfied customer.

Accurate replies, not more and not less, to questions you understand can add to your success.

Truth

"Those who exaggerate belittle themselves."
Frank Petrini 1900-1994

A sincere interest in people is accompanied by a strong desire to not mislead them in the slightest degree.

A quotation from the Talmud reads, "If you add to the truth you subtract from it."

I wish every person selling anything would implant that truth in his or her mind.

When you paint the picture a little better than it really is, in effect, you make it worse than it really is. Maybe not at that very moment; but you do when the buyer finds out that the product doesn't quite meet the picture you presented. And, ultimately, he or she will find out.

Why is that? Won't the buyers recognize that they got almost all that was promised? Won't they just shrug off the slight exaggeration -- the "salesman's license"? No, they won't!

On the contrary, buyers will think only about the shortfalls. Their attention will focus on the disappointment. They will think only about the benefit they thought they were going to receive but didn't get.

Haven't you had personal experiences of this kind when you were the buyer instead of the seller?

Some years ago, I bought a new car. In going over the list of features we wanted on the car, both my wife and I are certain we got an affirmative answer when we asked about a trunk lid release button. At that time, trunk release buttons were relatively uncommon. When the car was delivered, it didn't have one.

A trunk lid release button is a small thing. Some people wouldn't pay ten cents to have one. But to me it is not unimportant. I like the convenience of being able to open the trunk without leaving the driver's seat.

When viewed as a part of the total car, the trunk release is insignificant. The car had a great engine, beautiful design, high quality finish, road-gripping tires, a lifetime battery, cruise control with memory, and many other fine features. But I expected all that. I also expected the trunk lid release button, and my irritation at getting less than expected overshadowed the pleasure of all the other, and admittedly more important, features.

Buyers expect to get all that is promised, or all that they think was promised. Even a slight omission is cause for irritation. An irritated customer is not the kind of buyer most sales representatives want.

Some salespeople try to hide behind the excuse, "But, I didn't say that was one of the features, the buyer just assumed it was." This is no better than the case where the sales representative knowingly promises more than will be delivered. An irritated customer is an irritated customer no matter what the cause.

If you suspected the customer's assumption, then you were wrong to not set him right. The fact that you did not say, "Sure you'll get that, too," is a thinly veiled excuse. The failure to correct a false impression is tantamount to telling the untruth yourself.

Some people have the erroneous belief that sales representatives are supposed to be untruthful -- that it is an expected part of the selling process to exaggerate benefits and to cover up shortcomings. When people harboring that belief become sales representatives, their conduct may be directed toward fulfilling their own misguided assumptions about salesmanship. The results can be disastrous.

I've known two such sales representatives. Both had Ph.D. degrees in science, you would judge both intelligent by common standards, and yet they both played loosely with the truth if they thought it would get an order. Their image of selling was so ingrained that coaching did not convert their behavior. They were asked to move on to other employment.

I have known scientists who developed into superb sales representatives, so this deformation is not necessarily part of the scientific makeup. There are others who share it. What is puzzling is the reason for it.

That which is whispered in your ear is more believable than that which is told to you in full voice. Maybe that is the reason.

If one person says, "I know John has led an unblemished life," and another whispers to you, "I know John has done some things he wouldn't want known," which of those two phrases are you most likely to repeat and believe? Perhaps someone whispered untruths about selling to the two departed salespeople. I don't know.

But I do know there is no legitimate "salesman's license." It doesn't exist. Not among sales representatives who want to thrive in their profession.

I can't improve on the Talmud. Remember: "If you add to the truth you subtract from it."

CHAPTER 3

CUSTOMER FOCUSED SELLING

"Genuine understanding is the beginning of progress."
Frank Petrini, 1900-1994

Summary: Many selling formulas have been proposed and used that purport to lead the buyer into buying, but the best formula is no formula at all.

Napoleon said, "If you want to motivate men, give them what they want."

If you want to motivate customers, sell them what they want.

There are many definitions of selling in the world today. Here is one. It is not original with me and I don't remember where I came across it: Selling is a process whereby the seller ascertains and activates the needs or wants of the buyer and satisfies these needs and wants to the mutual, continuous advantage of both the buyer and the seller.

That covers the subject. However, could you give that definition to a newly hired sales trainee and expect him or her to take it from there without further instruction and help? You might, in a few rare cases.

Selling Formulas

I don't know who invented the selling formula AIDA, nor when it was invented. It has been around for decades. The acronym stands for Attention, Interest, Desire, Action.

The centerpiece of AIDA is a sales presentation. The sales representative makes the presentation to a buyer using words and visuals designed to grab the buyer's attention, then convert that attention to interest. The next step, of course, is to develop the interest into desire and reinforce the desire with conviction. The action, the final step, may mean getting the buyer's signature on an order or perhaps immediately trading product for compensation.

If the salesperson can't prepare such a presentation, there is an eager sales manager ready to do it.

This formula for selling is convenient -- you need only one presentation. Just get the right words in the right sequence drilled into your brain and, if you deliver with the proper degree of enthusiasm, whatever that is, you will always come out with an order. Well, not always.

I know a sales manager who declares that the only thing of importance in selling is enthusiasm. I always smile and say nothing because my personal feeling is negative toward highly enthusiastic sellers. "Is this enthusiasm trying to mask the facts?" I ask myself.

I can testify to the success of AIDA, in certain circumstances. I can testify because I have become a buyer at the hands more than one person using the AIDA formula. I have bought cutlery, car wax, and household cleansers because of several "gee whiz" sales presentations. In each of these cases, the monetary expenditure was modest and I figured I would never see the sales representative again.

The weakness in AIDA is the that there is little place for buyers to talk. You never learn anything about the idiosyncrasies of their business nor about their individual needs. If product is sold, it is largely hit or miss and requires a huge number of fresh prospects.

Presentations are still the way of selling for many because it seemingly means less work. It doesn't strain the mind. The buyer adjusts to you, not you to the buyer. You don't have to ask questions that can lead to uncharted waters; into areas where you are not comfortable.

If you are selling a low cost product, are here today and gone tomorrow (probably forever), AIDA may be a useful formula to follow. However, if your business relies on repeat sales and the positive recommendation of satisfied customers, there is a more productive way to sell.

Proposal Selling

Proposal selling comprises these steps: conditions, proposal, how-it-works, results, and next step. All the steps may not necessarily happen on one sales call. They could, but often they may stretch over several calls. This is particularly true with the development of the conditions.

In the "conditions" phase you guide buyers into describing and agreeing on conditions and/or needs surrounding their particular situation. The conditions represent some level of dissatisfaction or discomfort which can be satisfied, relieved, or overcome with your product. You then "propose" the solution to these conditions and needs. That solution is your product. The "how-it-works" expands on that solution by describing, in whatever detail necessary, the implementation of the solution. The "results" are a statement of the benefits matched to the buyer's previously agreed conditions and needs. The "next step" is either a signature on an order or agreement on some action that eventually leads to an order.

You Can Use Proposal Selling To Your Advantage

The elements of proposal selling are faultless, but require skill, patience, and practice to perfect. Perhaps the most difficult element is establishing the conditions. You can't tell buyers what their conditions and needs are. You have to let them tell you in their own words and at their own pace. In most of the conversations you will have to prime the pump with open-ended questions (questions which cannot be answered by "yes" or "no"). You may also have to say, "Tell me more," or questions like "Why is that?" or "What does that do for you?" or "What is the reason for it?" and other questions that fit the situation.

While buyers talk, you focus on what is being said. You listen carefully and without judgment. You maintain eye contact and are not distracted by extraneous sights and sounds in your surroundings. You ask questions for clarification and restate responses to insure understanding. And you take notes. Why? There are four significant reasons:

1. You give importance to the buyers words -- a form of respect.
2. When people see you recording their words, the statements are more likely to be accurate.
3. You will not remember everything the buyer says. Notes will be useful in analyzing the conditions and needs and in summarizing what was said before stating your proposal. That is particularly true

where the proposal comes days or weeks after the development of the conditions.

4. In most cases you will be calling on this buyer repeatedly. A permanent record of what she or he told you in this and later interviews will be useful to you over time and indispensable to a successor should you turn over the business to another person.

The conversation between you and the buyer follows no set pattern, unless you wish to call "letting the buyer do all the talking" a pattern. Except for your questions, you do, indeed, let the buyer do the talking.

Keep in mind, as the buyer talks, that his or her needs must meet three qualifications:

1. You can provide the means to satisfy the needs.
2. You can gain understanding and agreement.
3. The needs must be important enough for the buyer to act.

When buyers finish their recitations and you do not elicit any further information with your questions, it is time to summarize what you think they said. Then, ask if your summary is accurate. If it is not, ask what changes would make it accurate. Then, when you both have the same understanding of the conditions of the situation and their business and personal needs, you can take either one of two directions.

One of directions is to say, "Goodbye. What I have to offer does not fit the conditions you have expressed. Thank you for telling me all about them." What you have to offer will not fit every situation or every buyer. Your first task is to find out if there is a fit and where there is not, cut it and get out. Your time, and the buyer's time, is too valuable to waste.

The second direction you can take, knowing you have the solution, is to ask the buyer for a commitment. You could say: "If I can propose a solution that meets these conditions and needs, do you have a budget? Are you ready to buy?" If the answer is affirmative to both questions, move to the next step. If the answer is negative to either question, you want to find out what conditions are in the way.

Money may be a road-block and, if it really is, is it not better to find out now than an hour, week, or month later? Your questions will quickly determine if it is a true objection or an excuse. "If the money were not a problem, would you buy?" is one question you might ask.

If buyers say they are not ready to buy, your questions to determine why will probably uncover doubts about whether you really have a valid solution. It is normal.

Now is the time to make your presentation. Do they want details about how it works? Do they want a demonstration, proof, or perhaps testimonials from other customers? What is it that will build their confidence and remove their doubts? Ask. Don't shoot in the dark -- it is a waste of time and potentially dangerous if you miscalculate what buyers are thinking. Furthermore, if buyers tell you what will remove their doubts, they are saying in essence, "Give me a satisfactory answer to that and we're ready to buy."

Having resolved all outstanding issues, buyers are now in a position to commit to the logical next step: an agreement to buy. Continuing in the spirit of collaboration which you have followed to this point, you may ask the buyers to tell you what they would like you to do next. Or you could suggest a plan of action. Whichever approach is followed, you and the buyers now move forward with confidence in a wise decision.

What you have done, of course, is to qualify the buyers as a perfect fit for what you are offering and you have done it primarily with their own words. In the dialogue, astute questioning and empathic listening facilitated a meeting of the minds. You led them along the path to the point where the momentum shifted to their side -- it was no longer you wanting to sell, but it was the buyers wanting to buy. That is professional selling. The sales you earn are satisfying and lasting, and the customers return with a smile to bring you more business.

That is not formula selling. It is the method of proposal selling, but there is no firm structure. It is just common social sense as well as selling sense. It is the way you would try to get your brother to adopt something you thought would be good for him.

Again, the key is the careful development of the conditions of the situation and the buyer's business and personal needs. The development is by the buyer, not by you. You catalyze the conversation with questions and summaries, but nothing more. If you have the right solution, you have come close to concluding the sale when the buyer stops talking and before you have begun to talk.

Throw away the formulas and keep your presentation in your briefcase until the buyer asks to see it. You will sell more and create more satisfied customers.

Be Professional

My father-in-law is a physician. When a patient arrives at

his office complaining of some condition, does he take the person into the presentation room and embark on a long dissertation on pain, complemented with charts of the human anatomy and the nature of physiology? Of course, not. If he did, patients would head for the door. He knows that each patient is there to seek relief from his or her unique condition.

After hearing the patient's initial comments, he begins a series of questions. "How long have you been in pain?" "Where does it hurt?" "What do you feel when I put pressure here?" "When did the pain begin?" "Have you been involved in any unusual physical activity?" The questioning continues until he has a clear picture of the problem and has formulated a solution.

Think about your relationship with your physician. If the doctor did not inquire about your condition, did not ask if you are allergic to any medications before writing a prescription, did not ask you about your medical history, you would think there is something seriously lacking. You would ask yourself if this doctor is really a professional person.

Why should your customers feel differently about you? You cannot interest them in generalized solutions to their problems anymore than your doctor can interest you in generalized solutions to your particular situation.

Emulate your doctor -- be professional.

Let The Buyer Ask You

Did you wonder a bit when you read the suggestion several paragraphs above that you let the buyer suggest what to do next? I wouldn't be surprised because it is unusual. Please don't discard it without trying it. You'll like the results. When buyers ask you to write the order, they are more firmly committed than when you ask them.

However, asking you to write the order might be too unusual for some buyers. Many career buyers have been conditioned to the sales representative asking for the order. They are not prepared to respond to the question, "What do you want me to do next?" They are not ready to say, "You might as well write up the order," and then respond to your next question, "Is that what you want me to do?" with a "Yes."

That exchange would never have taken place with one hard-nosed, career buyer I remember. I was selling a commodity and was not his sole supplier. I kept records of his purchasing patterns. When the records showed he had to be close to buying, I would contact him either by telephone or in a personal visit. On one memorable occasion, when my records indicated he was about ready to buy, I went to see him at his office.

We exchanged a few amenities and discussed generalities of the industry before I asked for an order. He turned me down. We digressed into some other subjects and in another five minutes I asked him, again. This time he said he had an ample supply and it would be a few weeks before he would be back in the market.

I said, "I've been tracking your use pattern and I know you need to buy now. Please give me an order."

He said, "OK, ship three 40 ton carloads, one a week for the next three weeks."

I thanked him and then asked, "Why didn't you give me this order the first two times I asked?"

He shot back, "You're a salesman aren't you? I think salesmen are supposed to work for their orders."

Personality Types

For many years, I have asked people what type of personality they expect in a salesperson. Whether I'm asking a professional buyer or an everyday consumer, the word I hear most often is "extrovert". It seems that people see the typical sales representative as someone who is outgoing, effusive, demonstrative, and talkative.

A few years ago I rode a ski lift to the top of a mountain with a salesman. In our twenty minute ride together, he told me how successful he was, how much money he was making, and how it had the sales "game" all figured out. He was outgoing, effusive, demonstrative, and very talkative. He fit the image of salespeople I've heard from so many customers.

If you turn to Webster's New World Dictionary, Second College Edition, you find these definitions:

Extrovert – a person whose interest is more in his environment and in other people than in himself.

Extroversion – an attitude in which a person directs his interest to things outside himself and to other persons rather than to his own experiences and feelings.

These definitions seem to fit the type person likely to fulfill the promise of a deep, genuine, and respectful interest in other people as discussed in the previous chapter, don't they?

However, winning salespeople place a high premium on qualities often attributed to those who are introverted: thoughtfulness, analytical ability, inquisitiveness, and highly developed listening skill. These are people who consciously put themselves in their customer's shoes. They ask questions, listen, and weigh the answers to fully develop the conditions their proposal must satisfy.

An extrovert, as defined by Webster, who blends these qualities often ascribed to an introvert, has the foundation for winning in sales.

Caring and Curious, Again

A few pages back I mentioned the characteristics I'd like to find in a salesperson, if I could have only two. My answer was caring and curious. I discussed caring; lets talk about curious.

Naturally curious people often don't have to hone their questioning skills. It is normal for them to ask questions and to delve for the meaning behind what they see and hear. It is not work for them to uncover their customers' situations and their buyers' needs and wants. On the contrary, it is an adventure.

People trained in scientific procedures often make good sales representatives. They have learned to be inquisitive, to question at every turn. They ask themselves, "Why did this happen?" "What caused this result?" "What could I do or say differently?" "Why did he respond the way he did?" "What is behind that particular position?"

Their curiosity is insatiable. They pursue the issue until they have the full understanding of the story. They know that the first response to a question does not always give the complete picture. They also know that until all the facts and emotions are exposed they cannot make a lasting fit between their product and a buyer's conditions, needs, and wants.

The nemesis of all sales representatives, if you can believe most of the writers, is cold calling. During my early training as a sales representative, my teacher, Gordon, told me this story about cold calling. To him, a curious person, a cold call was an exciting adventure.

When he was pounding the sidewalks of Chicago selling an array of chemicals, prospective customers were unlimited. Chicago abounded in small and medium size manufacturers and most of them needed a chemical intermediate or chemical assistance of some kind. If his product couldn't fill their need, maybe one of his customers' products could -- then he made two friends.

Gordon saved his cold calls for the end of the day and had discovered early in his years on the Chicago beat that cold calls were fun -- fun of discovery.

By making the cold call -- one a day -- the last call of the day, he could go home in high spirits.

The number of sales he made on that last call of the day -- a bonus call, if you will -- were much greater than he expected. After a while, he analyzed this phenomenon and decided it was for these reasons:

- His attitude was positive. He knew he liked cold calls and went into the establishment expecting the joy of discovery.
- He was relaxed. Because it was a bonus call, he felt no pressure to make a sale.
- The prospects were usually surprised to see a salesperson so late in the day and that created a favorable reaction. They were winding down their day and had time to talk about their business -- a favorite subject anyway.

Whether for those reasons or others, making cold calls became a game and a successful one. Gordon wasn't born with curiosity -- it was not innate. A chemistry teacher, whom he admired enormously, had taught him to be curious. You wouldn't think of chemical laboratory training as being applicable to salesmanship, but here was a direct link.

Curiosity is a valuable trait for a salesperson. If you are not naturally curious, you can train yourself to become curious. What do you need to know about the prospect and his business to determine if there is a fit for your product? List the items and follow each item with a question or questions that will elicit the information you need. Memorize the questions or write them on the call agenda card I'll discuss later.

If you will write the questions in the quiet of an evening when you are preparing for your calls the next day, it will be much easier than waiting until you are in front of the prospect to formulate the questions. After a few weeks you'll be so in the habit of asking the right questions you won't have to write them in advance of the call.

Cold calls don't have to be the bane of your day. They can be an adventure and you can make them so. Why don't you do it?

A Print Shop Example

The owner of a small printing plant and I had an interesting conversation about selling one day. Our talk began when he asked, "What can I say when a prospect says to me, `The printing I'm getting now satisfies me.'? I don't know what words to use next. It looks like he's slamming the door."

First, realize that this response is what you should expect. If the current printer wasn't satisfactory, the buyer would be out looking for you instead of you looking for him.

You can try a number of openings. Here's one:

"You would have surprised me Mr. Buyer, if you had said anything else."

Get the buyer's name into your first sentence -- people love to hear their name. However, don't overdo it. It has to sound natural.

Then ask questions that permit the prospect to talk and form a target of conditions, needs, and wants. You can't see the target until the prospect defines it as a result of your questions.

Here's another opening:

"Of course you are satisfied Mr. Buyer, it is only natural. However, you don't know how much better it could be because you haven't experienced our work." Then start asking questions.

And, here's one more:

"Mr. Buyer, you have no reason not to be satisfied until someone comes along to show you something else. That's why I'm here." Then start asking questions.

At this point, after the opening statement, many salespeople will say, "Let me show you . . ."

Surprise the buyer. Don't say that. Instead, say "May I ask you a few questions?"

You will intrigue the buyer with an approach he or she rarely, if ever, sees. Most buyers will answer, "Yes." To the few who answer, "No," you might ask one more question, "Why?" If the buyer still does not respond, politely leave until another day.

Let's talk about your questions.

The questions you might ask are endless and will vary with the particular circumstances and your sense of direction. Usually, you will start with general questions and become more specific as the conversation progresses.

"Could I please see some examples of recent printing you have had done?"

"What do you think about this piece of work?"

Be cautious about finding fault. The buyer bought it and without question, you do not wish to imply what-a-stupid-purchase-you-made.

If you are looking at a really fine printing job, say so. Honesty always rates high and earns respect.

"How many printers do you use now?"

"How do you pick one over the other for a particular job?"

"When was the last time you changed printers and what was the reason for the change?"

"How much lead time do you give your printers?"

"Do they usually produce within the agreed time?"

"What is uppermost in your mind when you place a printing order? What are your main concerns?"

Now you are finding out what is important to the buyer. This knowledge will help you decide if you can satisfy him or not. If you think you can, you also may have picked up some ideas about where you can excel. You can now direct his attention to specific jobs you might do for him.

"When do you expect to repeat this job or to have another one we can look at?"

"The price? I don't know until I talk to my paper supplier and you tell me the quantity you will need."

"How many of this piece did you have printed the last

time? What was the price for that?"

"Why do I want to know the price you paid? Because I may congratulate you and not take up more of your or my time. However, if I can produce equal or better quality and deliver it when you want it at a fair price, I'd like to give you the chance to try us out."

If the buyer won't willingly tell you the price paid for the printing job, don't push it. Some will and some won't. However, buyers will admire you for asking. Your stock will rise as they see you as a mature, level-headed business person.

The important point is to ask, ask, ask. Get the prospects to talk about their business, their work, their plans, their needs, their wants. Don't make it sound like an interrogation, but keep the focus on drawing out information.

Selling is easier this way. Many people don't enjoy listening, but like to talk instead. You do the listening and let the prospects do the talking. Telling isn't selling. Most prospects will sell themselves, if you gently guide the conversation and let them talk long enough.

At some point in this exchange, buyers may ask to see samples of your printing. Carry an assortment in your briefcase showing the range of your capabilities. However, do not under any circumstance display your printing samples unless the buyer asks to see them.

That's a tough rule to follow. Show-and-tell was part of our elementary school training and, if you were trained as a salesperson in the AIDA formula, it was part of that, too. You are proud of the printing your shop turns out and it is only natural to want to show it off. You should be proud of it. Show it, but not until the buyer asks to see it.

Did I hear you say you have gotten printing orders

simply by displaying your work? I'm sure you have. However, it was strictly hit or miss. Some buyers looked at it and turned their back. Others feigned interest and said, "Leave your card." If one out of 10 showed true interest, you were lucky. If one out 20 gave you a trial order, you were most fortunate.

Is that the kind of living you want? Will that buy the home you'd like to have and put your children through college? No, it won't.

If you want to earn top income as a seller of printing or whatever your product, adopt and practice proposal selling. Develop *conditions*, *needs* and *wants* through astute questioning and careful listening. State your solution, your *proposal*, and then accept the order. Don't display your printing samples unless the buyer asks to see them. Follow this method and you'll improve your selling success.

Benefit Reserve

Photographers always take more film than they expect to use. Who wants to sight the best photo opportunity of the day after the last frame of the last roll has been shot?

When you go fishing, you may take only one rod, but you always carry extra line, more than enough hooks, and ample bait or lures to have some left over when fatigue or darkness dictate the end of the day. When you have found the best spot on the water, who wants to be forced to quit for lack of bait or a lure?

When you go selling, do you likewise hold something in reserve? Or, do you expose the last frame or cast the last lure before you ask for the order?

I don't know what you do. But, I know what most

salespeople do. They tell it all. They spray the buyer with a scattergun of every conceivable benefit of their product or proposition. There is nothing held back. After all, it is easier to tell it all than to pinpoint the benefits most appealing to the buyer.

After the salesperson has told it all, what more can be done if the buyer says "No"? To what do you turn if you have run out the string? Maybe the benefits could be recited one more time. Occasionally it works.

But wouldn't it be better to have benefits in reserve? If you tell it all and still don't get the order, there is not much more you can do. Reserve benefits give you another chance   several more chances, one after the other.

When I've recited all the features of my product and translated them into benefits for the buyer, I feel like I'm standing in front of the customer completely nude. Vulnerable, very vulnerable. It is an extremely uncomfortable feeling. What am I going to do or say next if the buyer doesn't agree to buy? I've backed myself into a corner.

Let's look at it from the customer's point of view. If the buyer is interested in only one of your product's benefits, why should he be made to suffer through a demonstration or recitation of all the benefits? He may even think, "But, I'm interested in only that one benefit, why should I pay for the other benefits, too?"

Furthermore, if you insist on telling it all, you may talk past the point at which the customer is ready to buy. You are risking loss of the order. If something less than all the benefits your product or service provides will satisfy the buyer's needs, don't explain all the other benefits. Get the order and leave.

How do you find out which benefits interest the buyer?

You ask. Maybe you don't ask directly, or maybe you do. But by one means or another you must uncover the conditions of the total situation and the particular needs of the buyer -- both personal and corporate.

You engage the buyers in conversation about their business and about their needs as they perceive them. All the while they are talking, and as your questions encourage them to talk on, you are searching your mind to find a fit between their needs and the benefits your product or service offers. If there are no fits, you terminate the exchange and depart.

But, if you have done your pre-call homework, you are likely to find items of benefit which do meet the needs of the buyer. Concentrate on those items. Demonstrate through words, pictures, or live examples how your benefits do, indeed, match the needs and conditions the buyer has already expressed.

Always have an arsenal of benefits. Be stingy with them. Expend them frugally. Make it your objective to finish the job, have the order in hand and still have a reserve of benefits in the arsenal. You'll feel a lot more comfortable. And you will get more orders.

Undersell

Is it a good selling technique to undersell your product a little bit?

Once I built a new home. There were many planning sessions with the architect and with the builder. All the details of construction were carefully catalogued. I was satisfied that I would receive high quality construction at a fair price.

I watched the progress of construction almost daily.

Just after the installation of the wallboard began, I noticed a printed square every few feet on the wallboard which read, "Factory Mutual Approved Building Material. Gypsum Wallboard Type FSW. Fire Resistance Classification Design. Manufactured to Meet ASTM Standard C36."

The next day I called the builder and pointed out that fire resistant wallboard was not listed in the material specifications and that it must be higher in cost. I asked why he was using it.

He replied that he had been able to arrange a deal with his supplier to get the fire-resistant wallboard at the same price as the lower quality, specified board. He thought I would be happy with the better quality and, even though his installers were complaining about the greater weight of the fire-resistant board, he wanted to deliver the advantage of this superior quality.

Was I happy? Absolutely. And perhaps as much so because he hadn't made a point of saying, "Look what I'm doing for you." I discovered it independently, as I suspect he knew would happen.

After that I stopped looking at the details of construction as carefully as before. The builder had earned my complete confidence. I recommended him to many of acquaintances.

Is it a good selling technique to undersell your product a little bit? It certainly is. It is if you want to build customer confidence and stay in business a long time.

There is nothing which will tie a customer to you more closely than to leave unmentioned some product benefit that he or she will discover alone. "And I got even more than I paid for," is a wonderful feeling for a buyer to have.

When the customer greets you with a warm smile and

a firm handshake on your next visit and mentions the extra benefit discovered, you can pass it off by saying, "I'm delighted you're happy and so pleased you noticed. Our company always tries to build a little extra value into the products we sell."

Then, get ready to write the next order.

Somewhat the same idea, or at least the same emotion, is involved in price estimates. If the buyer says, "How much do you think this is going to cost?" the tendency of some sellers is to state a low price. They fail to mention extras necessary to the operation of the equipment, or installation, or freight or some other cost item. So when the final invoice is presented the buyer feels a pang of disappointment, if not irritation. The next sales call may not go as smoothly as the salesperson would like.

Put on your own buying shoes for a minute. When you take your automobile for repairs, it is common to ask the manager, "What will these repairs cost?" When you go back in the evening to recover the car and pay for it, you find, invariably, the bill is more than the estimate given that morning. Furthermore, the manager and mechanic have already left for the day so you can't question them. The cashier responds to your complaint with, "I'm just the cashier. If you want to pick up your car now, this is what you must pay." How do you feel at that moment, and even for the next few days?

Contrast that with your feelings on the rare day when you went for your repaired car and were told the bill was exactly the figure you were quoted in the morning or even a little less. You felt pretty good, didn't you? You wanted to thank the manager and mechanic and were sorry they were gone for the day.

Sellers use more mind than emotion, but buyers use

more emotion than mind. It is hard for buyers to admit this, but it is true. You just admitted your own emotional reaction to the two car repair situations. You were then the buyer. When you are selling, your buyers are susceptible to the same emotions you have when you are buying. That's a concept worth remembering!

And remember, also, when you give a buyer a price estimate always make it exact, or a little higher than it may be in the end. The resulting emotions will be in your favor.

Underselling, whether in benefits or in price, is a sound principle, understood by professional sellers and regularly employed by those most confident and competent.

Take Care Of It Yourself

There are subtleties in selling. Each, in itself, does not make a big difference but, in total, they do make a difference -- at least they do in the hands of a professional.

One of these subtleties has to do with positioning yourself in the mind of customers as the one person in your organization who can answer all their needs.

There may be times and circumstances when salespeople want to impress the customer with the depth of talent in their organization. In those cases it might be helpful to mention other people who back them up.

In most circumstances, however, sales representatives serve their purposes best by creating the image of personally orchestrating the entire relationship between the company that is buying and the company that is selling.

If the buyer says, "We'll need more complete engineering data on the new product you're proposing," the proper response is, "I'll get it for you," -- not, "I'll have our engineering department send it to you." If you say

say that, you seem less important and less necessary to the customer.

If the buyer asks, "Can I stretch your thirty-day terms to forty-five days?" the preferable response is, "No, credit terms are firm." You would not say, "I don't know but I'll ask our credit manager." Why? Because it is your territory, your customer, your business. You run it, operate it, and call the shots.

If the buyer says, "You are about to lose my business because your last three shipments have been late," how does a professional respond? Don't say "I'll check with the shipping department and find out what's wrong." The only acceptable answer is "I'm sorry, I'll see it doesn't happen again. When would you like the next shipment to arrive?"

The customer doesn't need to know who a sales representative contacts to get information or to make things happen. If the specialists in engineering, manufacturing, credit, or shipping are going to solve all the customer's problems and satisfy all desires, then why does the customer need a salesperson?

In the back of their minds, customers know the sales representative goes to company specialists to get answers. But they want the sales representative to be a dynamic, take-charge type person who can make things happen within the company, and make them happen for the customer's benefit.

When sellers say, "I'll have to get the information from our marketing people," they tarnish the image of the I-can-do-it-for-you individual. The buyers want you to say, "I'll take care of it." "I'll do it for you." "Just leave it to me." "Yes we can," or even, "No we can't."

Do you believe it? Think of this. You've bought an automobile, probably several. In those situations you were the buyer, the other person was the seller. How did you feel about the salesperson who said, "Let me talk to our sales manager about this"?

I know an automobile salesman who does not say that. "When price is discussed he doesn't say, "Let me talk to the sales manager and see what I can do." If it is a service question he doesn't say, "I'll have to talk to the service manager about that." What he does say is, "This is the price and it is the best I can do." To a service inquiry he'll say, "I'll find out," or, "I'll do it."

There are ten salespeople where this person works and he personally sells forty percent of the cars.

It is a subtle thing but it is real. His customers have a warm, comfortable feeling of confidence and they keep coming back to him.

Be the kind of sales representative your customer wants you to be -- *you* take care of it. The customer doesn't care how you do it nor to whom you talk. Just do it and don't say how. It is one of those small things, which when done well, contributes to selling success.

Prove The Case

Product and service publicity stories, also called case histories, can be a valuable adjunct to other activities (advertising, sales literature, direct mail, sales calls, etc.) in the marketing program mix. Do you get them? Do you use them?

You can build an incisive proposal for customers and prospects. You can meticulously take them through the steps of whatever selling process you use -- every step which leads in logical progression to the final "ask for the order" -- and all the while the customer will be thinking,

"As great as it sounds, I wish I could see proof."

Case histories provide the proof. They can convert doubt to conviction. They can increase your chances of getting the customer's or prospect's signature on the order when you get to that concluding step.

You obtain case histories in the normal course of your sales work. Every salesperson is exposed to happy customers, customers who are pleased to tell you how they used your product or service, why it worked well for them, and what benefits they derived from it. You hear these stories all the time.

If you are attuned to the value of these success stories you also will be ready to record them. You can flesh them out with a little more detail and develop a factual case history that can be used as a convincing sales tool with first-time buyers.

Chances are that your best candidates for publicity stories are among your satisfied customers, people you have called upon a number of times. You have a large part of the information either on record or in your head. To complete the story you don't have to run through a long list of questions; but simply fill in the missing pieces.

You might say, "I wasn't trained in journalism, so how do I know what information is needed for a reasonably good case history or publicity story?" It is not difficult. Just think of yourself as the reader of a story. What would you want to know? The five W's of journalism are who, what, where, when, and why.

Who is (was) involved? Stories about people have high reader interest. People like to read about people. So, get names up front.

What is it about or what happened? A logical next step. "Who did what" combines the first two W's.

Where was it done or where did the action take place? Who did what, where? People are always more interested in local events than in something far away. If your neighbor's house burns down it is big news. If a house burns down in a town a hundred miles away, you may never hear about it. Early in the story they want to know where it happened.

Next answer the question "when." Is your story about the future, present or past? Be specific -- readers want to know. Your neighbor's house burning is big news the day it happens and no news at all a few weeks later.

Why did it happen? Or, why did this particular "who" get involved in this "what " which took place or will take place "where" and "when"?

Now you get down to some of the apple slices under the pie crust. An extension of "why" is "how." The amount of space you give to why and how will depend on your judgment of how interesting the story is. But, it is far better to have too much than too little. If you have too much you can always edit out part of it. If you have too little it may be difficult, and sometimes impossible, to go back to the story source for more facts.

It could be useful to draw up a form listing twenty or more questions which will give you a complete story.

Better to think it through in advance than to depend upon memory or intuition at the site.

Who are you interviewing? Who else is involved? What is the business name and address? How long has it been established? Are titles of interest? What is the education and/or experience of each participant? How long have they been involved?

What product or service was used? Why was it used or what was the need which precipitated this use? Was it used alone or in combination with other things? Where and when was it used? How was it used -- get details.

Whose idea was it? Who was involved in planning, in evaluation of results?

What problems were solved? What were the results? Why was it better than before? Cost? Performance? What are the plans for future use?

There may be other facts you wish to gather or other questions you wish to explore appropriate to your particular product or service. Having a prepared list will be helpful and maybe even necessary until you have had the experience of researching and writing a few stories. You do not have to be a journalist to do a good job on a publicity story. It is a logical extension of selling. The questions you ask, the story you put together is what a professional salesperson would be doing anyway.

The old saying, "A picture is worth a thousand words" is not literally true. Pictures are valuable but you still need words. Pictures *and* words are best. Here are some picture possibilities: the people; the home or place of business; your product or service at the time and place of use; if equipment is involved in the use, show that; and 'the end result.

You can use pictures in a variety of ways. If one of your objectives is to have the story published in a newspaper or magazine you will enhance that possibility when the story is accompanied by one or more pictures. Editors love pictures.

There are many obvious uses for pictures. But one that is sometimes overlooked is to give copies of photographs back to your source. Most people like to have pictures of themselves, their establishment, and equipment. If you have an especially good picture, have it blown up to 8" x

10" and frame it. It is a nice, low cost way to say thank you for the story.

Variety and interest are heightened in any story if it includes quotations from the person interviewed. Most people will give you time to write their exact words. They are flattered you want to do so.

It is wise to take the final story and pictures back to the source to check for accuracy and get a signed approval for whatever use you plan to make of them. When you have included identified quotations in the story, it is a necessity that pre-publication approval be obtained.

If your story is to be used beyond your own territory or in a public media, your company, large or small, has a procedure for publicity story approval. There are sound reasons for it. Make sure you know what that procedure is and follow it.

How will you use publicity stories and case histories? There are multiple possibilities.

In their simplest form you can have them typed and stapled individually for your personal use on sales calls, as meeting handouts, or in mailings.

Taking this one step further you could put a number of related stories in a binder. Use them as opportunity dictates. They will be a supplement to your sales proposal, not a substitute. They provide the proof you didn't have before. You won't always need them. Every prospect does not ask for proof. But it is comfortable to have them in your briefcase when you need proof to help sell your product.

Moving up one more step, you can improve the production quality by taking your story and pictures to a print shop and having them lay it out and print it in a visually attractive way. This story then may find even broader use in your territory and other territories. Selective mailing is an additional use you will probably make of this upgraded piece.

Finally, you may choose to submit your story for publication to an appropriate magazine or newspaper, which will gain broad exposure. Magazines will usually be happy to sell you reprints of published articles at nominal cost. These reprints can then be used in any or all of the ways already suggested -- for sales calls, for handouts at meetings or conventions, and for either selective or broad mailings. Published case histories carry a high degree of acceptance and credibility.

Case histories or publicity stories (call them what you will) can be valuable to every seller. They provide evidence of proof that some buyers want. Furthermore, it is a fun way to sell.

"Don't just take my word for it. Look at what happened in these actual cases," you might say while presenting the proof which will seal the sale.

Silent Selling

"Silence is the sacred pathway to wisdom."
    Frank Petrini, 1900-1994

On several occasions, I accompanied top executives of my company as they called on top executives of other companies.

Although my role was more chauffeur than anything else, I was able to sit at the table with them as they were negotiating a sale and a purchase.

The people involved on both sides of the negotiations were not the same in each case and the type of business at stake differed. The one thing in common among all the people in all the situations was that they were mature, experienced businesspersons. They had been negotiators a long time.

Another thing which was common in all three of these selling-buying sessions was silence -- long periods of silence.

Silence in selling was unique in my experiences up to that point, so I was particularly sensitive to what I was observing at those negotiating tables. As a matter of fact, on my first exposure, not being prepared for something which seemed unusual, I was uncomfortable with the silence. And even though I was only an onlooker, it was difficult to contain the urge to jump into the silence and say something.

But then I noticed these seasoned professionals were not uncomfortable with their silence. I recall on one occasion a negotiator sat with his elbows on the table and his head in his hands. It was clearly his turn to say something and when nothing was said for what seemed like an interminably long time, I thought the man had fallen asleep.

Of course, there were periods of rapid exchange and continual conversation, too. But from time to time a question or a statement designed to elicit a response would elicit nothing more than a reflective expression -- an appearance of saying, "Wait a second." Or the person might audibly mutter, "Let me think about that a minute."

The significant thing in these situations, one might even say the interesting thing to the novice, was that neither party in the negotiations thought that silence was strange. Neither person was uncomfortable with periods of thinking, periods when no words were spoken, periods of silence. On the contrary it seemed natural and normal -- it did to them. There was not the slightest indication of embarrassment nor of being uncomfortable.

And that, I submit, is in sharp contrast to most negotiators, who are terrified by silence or, if not, they at least give a credible imitation of someone who is. So let's ask the question: In a buying-selling situation, in negotiations, if you prefer, what is wrong with periods of silence? "Nothing," you say. And I would agree. Yet it is curious why there is so little silence in sales; why we often hear sales representatives putting words in buyers' mouths.

How many times have you heard or been part of a conversation somewhat like this:

Seller: "How has business been over the past three months?" "Up? "Down?" . . . "Steady?"
Buyer: "Yep."
Seller: "What do you think the reason is?" . . . "The general economic climate?" . . . "The floods in the Mississippi Valley?" . . . "Grain export levels?"
Buyer: "I guess so."
Seller: "In view of that, do you want to order today? Or, would some time in the future be better?
Buyer: "The future is fine."

Is this an exaggeration? Not in the least.

And so the seller files a report on this call, writing: "Buyer's business has been steady over the past three months. He attributes this to the general economic climate and will be ready to order again in the near future."

Is that what the buyer said? Of course not! The buyer didn't say anything. Sure, he uttered a few sounds, but he

didn't say anything.
Let's try it again.

> *Seller:* "How has business been over the past three months?" **(Silence!)**
> *Buyer:* "Our business has been relatively good."
> *Seller:* "To what do you attribute that?" **(Silence!)**
> *Buyer:* "Well, the general economic level is not bad, and we have been helped by the surge in grain exports."
> *Seller:* "In view of that, you must be ready to place another órder. Do you want delivery this week or next?" **(Silence!)**
> *Buyer:* "I don't know. Let me check my inventory sheets." **(Silence!)** "If you could have a shipment in here by the end of next week, that would be fine."
> *Seller:* "It will be here. Thank you very much."

There are a number of reasons why silence in selling is smart; reasons why it not only makes sound sense, but why it is a positive aid to the successful conclusion of a sale. Let's discuss some of these reasons:

Silence is polite

It is common courtesy to give people the chance to answer a question in their own words. When faced with those who compulsively answers their own questions, I have at times been motivated to interrupt with, "Do you wish to know my answer to the question or do you prefer to continue telling me what you think I think?" Of course, that usually brings the monologue to a halt. Then it is interesting to note the surprised expression when they find my point of view is distinctly different from the one they were formulating for me.

But, sadly, one reproach does not stop haters of silence. Tentative responses to their own questions have become a habit. They are right back at it within seconds. It is automatic. They are not even aware of their rudeness.

Silence is polite and most buyers, if given a choice, would prefer to buy from polite sellers.

Silence invites response

If you ask a question, you should want an answer. If you do not want an answer, don't ask the question. Nothing is more aggravating than a person filling voids with pointless, meaningless questions.

So, let's assume that when you ask a question you want an answer. Some buyers in some situations may be reluctant to give you an answer. By posing tentative responses to your own question, you are taking them off the hook -- you are giving them a multiple-choice quiz. The buyer will pick the answer that is least controversial; the one he or she guesses will best satisfy you. You provide an easy way for the buyer to avoid giving a direct answer to your question.

However, if the question is followed by silence, the buyer has no choice; the question must be answered. Now you will begin to discover the facts which lead you to match the needs with the benefits you offer.

The only way a seller can achieve his or her objective is to get the buyer to talk. And the buyer will talk only when the seller is silent. Ask the question and then be still. Silence facilitates a response.

Silence gives thinking time

Some people think more quickly than others. Some answers require more thought than others. If you ask a question you want an answer. Isn't a thoughtful answer more valuable to you than a thoughtless one? As a matter of fact, if you are down to the last question -- "Will you give me the order?" -- and if you don't give the buyer time to weigh the points for and against the purchase, you are more likely to get a negative than a positive response. It is an axiom of management practice that when forced into a quick decision, always say "No"; you will be right more often than not.

So, you want an answer and you want a thoughtful answer. The only way to get it is to give the buyer time to think. Learn to be comfortable with silence, even sixty seconds of it.

Silence is polite. Silence invites response. Silence gives thinking time. Silence increases sales. Yet it is an accurate observation -- test it yourself -- that fear of silence or, at least, a lack of comfort with silence, is pervasive in all social and business intercourse.

Learn to be comfortable with silence, and your sales will grow.

Expectations Vs. Reality

Ninety-nine percent of the problems in interpersonal relations can be attributed to the variance between expectations and reality.

How many marriages do you know that were dissolved because of the variance between expectations and reality? He expected children; in reality she didn't want children. She expected an equitable distribution of his attention between her needs and his business; the reality was that if the business were to survive it took all of his attention. He expected a full-time housekeeper and cook; in reality she liked neither and planned to finish her college degree and then work.

The physical attraction between a man and woman make them both poor analysts and poor listeners. They don't take time nor thought to list their expectations and compare them. And so when the truth of the variances between each of their expectations begins to emerge -- the reality one perceives doesn't match the expectation of the other -- the union begins to dissolve. It can only be saved by compromise.

Customers are not like husbands and wives. In many cases there is no contractual union between buyer and seller. It is far, far easier to discard a seller than it is to divorce a mate.

But customers are just like husbands and wives -- like all of us -- in their susceptibility to frustration, to irritation, even to anger when there is a variance between expectations and reality.

What is the lesson for salespeople? It's simply this: don't promise more than you can give. Or, conversely, make sure you give all you promise.

But it isn't quite that easy. Because what a seller thinks is said or implied and what the listener thinks is said or implied are often poles apart.

So, you have to explore the buyer's perception, the expectations of what the product or service being sold will do. You have to question to make sure that what the buyer expects and what will be delivered are exactly matched. Did the buyer fully understand your proposition and the results promised?

If a variance exists between the buyer's expectations and the reality of what you will deliver, there must be an adjustment to avoid a problem -- a dissatisfied customer. Either the buyer must adjust his expectations to the reality of what you will deliver or you must adjust what you will deliver to meet the buyer's expectations.

There is no other choice. If you are to be a successful salesperson, buyer *expectations* and the *reality* of your delivery must *match*.

Canned Is Better Than Rotten

Who would not recognize that a ripe Alberta, picked in the late summer from a mature, carefully nurtured tree and eaten immediately, is the juiciest, most succulent peach a person could hope to enjoy?

So, why do we can peaches? Because peaches spoil rapidly if not canned or frozen. Furthermore, not only are there too many to eat in a short period of time, but a canned peach is still pretty good eating, and canned is certainly better than rotten.

Among sales representatives there is a universal cry against the canned sales presentation and the canned speech. "You can't use another person's words and make them sound like your own," it is often said.

You can't? Do you deny the existence of Gene Hackman, of Sissy Spacek, of Glenn Close, of Robert DeNiro, of countless performers who are playing in theaters and cinemas around the world every hour of the day and night?

You probably cannot name one thing any of these artists wrote, but you may remember many things each of them said -- and not a word of it was their own. They did not write their own stuff; certainly they did not speak extemporaneously. What did they do? They memorized words written by Shakespeare, by Moliere, by Simon, by Faulkner, by Miller, by Hammerstein and by many other playwrights and screenwriters.

"But," you retort, "I'm not an actor. A sales representative is not an actor, never is and never was supposed to be." If that is your response, I'll debate with you.

First of all, I'll agree with you partially. When you were offered employment as a salesperson nobody ever said anything about the responsibility of being an actor -- that was not part of the job description. There are, however, elements of dramatization in your work, opportunities for achieving a goal by using the skills of an actor or an actress.

Here are two quotations that might be in a sales representative's job description:

"The primary responsibility is to sell products and to employ skills consistent with good selling practices to attain this end."

"To organize and conduct meetings for retailers and consumers to influence them to place orders for our products."

Let's take each of these and see how acting could apply -- even more how it is applied by the cream of sales representatives, the top professionals.

If you are going to "employ skills consistent with good selling practices," that means, among other things, that you study the buyers to whom you sell. You note their likes and dislikes, you observe their dress, you watch their reactions to your demeanor and to your words so that, over a period of time, you build a personal profile of each buyer and you consciously adjust your dress, your behavior, your words to gain approval. Is that not acting?

Today you saw eight different buyers. Each buyer was a different personality. One expects to hear your latest joke. One doesn't like jokes at all. One enjoys being taken to lunch. One would rather take you to lunch. One is a great decision-maker whom you subtly lead to make the decision you want. One cannot make a decision, and you have to almost force the pen into his hand and guide his signature on your order pad. One buyer reacts positively to meekness. Another buyer detests a meek salesperson.

A salesperson could visit all of these different buyers within one day. You have to make adjustments to accommodate the personalities, the idiosyncrasies of the buyers' if you want to earn their business.

Is this not acting? Of course it is!

I heard a rebuttal once that was about like this: "No, I do not adjust to the buyer at all. I have carefully developed my own character, my own personality, my approach, and I stick with that. I'm comfortable with it, and I'm successful with it."

If that is your answer, you are in the majority -- a very large majority of all salespeople. But, if that is your answer you are not as successful as you might otherwise be. You are missing some business that could be yours.

Do you rebel at the thought of a canned sales presentation? Some sales representatives do. I do too, if by "canned" it is something written to be recited as a monologue without benefit of customer questions or comments. That kind of canned sales talk is patently and transparently unnatural. No salesperson likes it; few customers respond positively to it, and it is ineffective. However, if a portion of the peach is rotten, don't you cut away the spoiled part and eat all the good which is left?

Some sellers have what might be called a "demi-canned" sales presentation. They developed it themselves through a combination of common sense and trial and error. They know, for example, if they want to elicit information from a customer, they avoid asking questions which can be answered merely by "yes" or "no." If you want information about future requirements, you don't ask, "will your requirements be up over the next 12 months?" What you do ask is, "how much will your requirements be over the next twelve months?"

To get the information they need, salespeople prepare questions in advance and mentally rehearse them. They do not wait until they are face-to-face with the customer, because for some inexplicable reason the questions you think up on the spur of the moment are more likely to be the closed-ended type, yielding limited information. Much better are the open-ended, illuminating variety, producing valuable information.

Frank Bettger, generally acknowledged as one of the leading insurance salesmen of the Twentieth Century, had a repertoire of questions and statements which he both borrowed from other successful sales representatives and developed on his own. He used them again and again, word for word, precisely in the way that produced the results he desired. Bettger wrote them down, he committed them to memory and he used these phrases because he got results with them. They were his "demi-canned sales presentation." What are your questions and phrases?

One sales representative, when asked to use a canned sales presentation, said this to me: "I am not going to use canned sales presentations, because they are not mine. I am no hypocrite. I'm my own person and I just wouldn't feel right using somebody else's material. It would bother my conscience."

I'm sympathetic with that point of view. If you can write great sales presentations, by all means do it. However, not everyone has that ability. Think about it this way: Nobody is really asking you to compromise your principles. But, be objective. If a canned sales presentation tells it better than you've been doing, why not adopt it as though it were your own and use it? Don't let pride stand in your way of getting the order.

The best sales representatives are "on stage" when they are with their customers. They are skillful actors and actresses. Of course, only *they* know they are acting (or their sales manager who observes their performances). It is never evident to the buyer.

Let's take the other job description: "To organize and conduct meetings for retailers, and consumers . . ." If your meeting is pure presentation -- no discussion, no questions and answers, and if you are not a natural born orator, you are forced into effective presentation techniques. (Acting!) You are forced into it, that is, if you want to sell. If you want the people in your audience to take some action as the result of your speech, you have to stimulate them. How do you stimulate them? The same way speakers stimulate you -- you know the difference between a good and bad speech when you are in the audience -- you use oratorical skills.

I know one salesperson who so meticulously built his

technical background, so completely analyzed his audiences, so thoroughly observed their reactions, and so skillfully prepared and rehearsed his speeches that no competitors would appear on the same program.

You might ask, "Why didn't the competitors develop a dynamic style of their own? Why didn't they learn some acting, too. Maybe it is laziness. Maybe it is assumed this salesperson's abilities are "natural," and they couldn't do as well, even if they tried. That is an easy cop-out. It's like people who say, "I'd give a year of my life if I could play the piano like that." They are lying. They wouldn't give even one hour for the first lesson. If they had worked as hard and as long studying the piano as the performer, then they would play it like a twin. But, they won't make the effort.

I know for a fact that the salesperson the others won't compete with on the podium worked long and hard to achieve superiority as a speaker. And while his acquired style is by now a part of him, he still spends hours preparing his words and visuals for every talk. What appears to be "natural" is simply the result of much dedicated time and effort. He is a true actor, and he sells a lot of product because he is an actor.

Not every sales representative has the word knowledge nor the oratory skill to pick the words and to string them together for maximum effect. If this is not one of your strengths, and if you do not wish to take the time to develop it as one of your strengths, then accept the speech written by a wordsmith and practice it until it sounds like your own, just like those who earn their living acting.

Whether it is a sales presentation or a speech, canned is better than an alternative not as good. Your objective is to inspire action, to get orders from a single person or from a room full of people. If you lack the inclination or the ability to develop your own material, to do your own play writing, then, at least, become an actor or actress.

You can effectively use another person's words, as do highly paid artists of the stage and screen, and get superior results. Canned peaches, are better than rotten. So are canned words.

Service After The Sale

If you are selling a single-use product with no opportunity for another order, maybe you don't have to think about service after the sale.

Most buyers, however, buy the same product, or a similar product repeatedly. Whether you get the repeat orders or your competitors get some or all of the orders is determined by several factors. One of these factors is the service you provide after the sale.

Was the shipment received on time? Was it in the condition you had promised? Is everything running smoothly in the use of your product? Do the production people need any technical help?

These are questions you can pose to the buyer over the telephone the day after the delivery was due to arrive. Even though he or she may not yet have the answers to all those questions, the fact that you called demonstrates respect, care, and rings very favorably with the buyer.

Buyers like back-up. They don't know all the technical details about the use of your product. If the second shift production superintendent calls at 9:00 p.m. to report problems with your product, the buyer needs to be able to reach you right now. Make sure your buyers have your home telephone number and assure them you are available twenty-four hours a day for backup.

That is the kind of service after the sale that will convert a satisfied customer into a delighted customer and keep you in the preferred supplier seat.

Customer Focused Selling

To achieve long-term customer satisfaction and repeat sales, presentations have their place, but they are not the centerpiece in the relationship between the buyer and sales representative. Customers and prospects, their unique conditions, needs and wants, are the centerpiece. You bring the sales presentation into play only after buyers have told you everything and together you have reached mutual agreement that you have a potential solution. The sales presentation, at that point, explains the details of your proposal and converts the interest in your solution into desire and conviction.

This is not a new concept. Sales trainers have been teaching and writing about customer focused selling for a long time. They may not use the exact same words, but the intent is parallel. In spite of this emphasis many sales representatives still pitch their product without asking even a few simple questions to determine the customers' needs and wants.

Why not lead the way in your business to throw the spotlight on your customers and prospects? You'll be more than satisfied, your customers will love it, and you'll be delighted with the results.

CHAPTER 4

DRIVE TO CONTACT MANY CUSTOMERS AND PROSPECTS

"What's behind the door, I cannot tell.
But this I know, and know it well.
The more I open, the more I sell!"
Author Unknown

Summary: Without sacrificing call quality, there are many ways to contact more customers and prospects.

When I was a beginning salesman, my territory was the eastern two-thirds of Missouri. I sold herbicides, products used by farmers to control weeds in their corn and soybean fields. The farmers purchased their herbicides from farm supply dealerships spread throughout the territory, usually one or two dealers to a town. Nearly two hundred such retail establishments existed within my territory.

I was the first DuPont salesperson to live in this territory. My predecessors had lived out of state and covered much larger areas. Because of the significantly greater geography they covered, each had been able to work with only the larger dealers. My challenge was to substantially increase market share. That meant calling on many dealerships and their farmer customers. To accomplish this required motivation, long hours, an enormous amount of time driving, and skillful use of time.

One fact I learned quickly was that not everyone had the same lunch hour. I remember arriving in a small town at noon, on my first round of calls, and saying to myself, "There's no use in trying to make this initial contact now. The person has surely gone to lunch or is about to leave."

I ate lunch by myself and arrived at the dealership a few minutes after 1 p.m. The receptionist said the person I wanted to see had just gone to lunch. So, I had another hour to kill -- no additional customers or prospects were in that town and it was a twenty minute drive to the nearest dealership.

Doing nothing for two hours was not my idea of a productive day. Furthermore, by the time I finished that call and drove to the next town, it might be too late for even one more call.

After a few experiences like that I began telephoning ahead when it got close to noon and asked the person I wanted to see when he planned to leave for lunch. If he was leaving at noon, I tried to get a lunch date and if it was a later hour I simply said I was on my way to see him and would be there in a few minutes. Following that routine, I was off to the next town by 1 p.m. or sooner and got in two or three more calls during the afternoon.

I then made it a practice to ask about the person's lunch habits the first time I called on someone. Many dealership managers went home for lunch at the same time each day. Whatever the individual's habit, I noted it on my master customer record card. That permitted me to plan accordingly on future trips.

Knowing customers' habits and planning around them resulted in less wasted hours and more hours for selling.

The Best Time To Make A Sales Call

There was a large, important dealership located in the far northeast corner of the territory, a three-hour drive from my home. Because the location was remote, I would plan my travel in order to stay in a motel about ten miles from the dealership. This allowed me to start the day with a call on the manager and work my way southward.

My appointments with the manager were always set for 8 a.m. While he received me politely, it was impossible to have a productive conversation. If it wasn't the telephone ringing it was subordinates coming in and out of his office making verbal reports or asking for instructions.

After several calls like that, I said to him, "It's obvious this is not a good time to see you. Is there another time when it would be more convenient for me to call? He looked at me with a twinkle in his eye and asked, "Do you mind getting up early?" I answered, "Of course not." And he said, "OK, then come in at six o'clock. That is when I arrive and I don't begin to get busy until seven. We can start the day together with a cup of coffee."

So, I started calling at the dealership at six. On the second call he turned from a prospect into a customer. It was a satisfying experience and taught me a good lesson. From then on whenever I sensed that my calling time was inappropriate, I always inquired if there was a better time to call. That simple question got me a lot of business.

You don't run into many competing sellers at 6 a.m. or 11 p.m. and if your customer is working then, you get to visit with no waiting and no distractions.

Have you ever heard salespeople say something like this: "I never make an office call before ten in the morning because until then they are busy with the morning mail."?

The persons who say that are ignoring common office practice. In many offices the mail is usually not distributed until mid-morning. Furthermore, with the electronic communication systems operating today, messages of importance are coming in over the telephone, computer, and fax machine all day long. There is no one time for mail.

Ask the people you call on regularly, "When is the best time to see you?" Many of the answers will surprise you. Often the time suggested will be at odd hours -- a time when you normally would not have been making calls. That is one easy way to see more customers and get more business, too.

When is the best time to make a sales call? The best time is when the customer or prospect wants to see you.

Other Ways To Make More Calls

Dividing your territory into geographical areas is one easy device to minimize driving and maximize calls. You work one trip area at a time. You can split a large country territory into states, parts of states or counties. A metropolitan territory can be split into postal zones.

If something comes up in a trip area other than the one where you are working, try substituting a telephone call for a personal visit. It often works as well, particularly with a customer you know.

Include some blank time slots in your plan. Then, if an unplanned diversion comes along, you can take care of it without destroying your total route planning.

Do you set goals for the number of calls you want to make? When I was working the territory in Northeast Missouri, my goal was to make three calls before noon.

When I met my morning goal the whole day turned out well and when I didn't meet it, even the afternoon tended to fall apart. I can't explain it, but I did document it.

There is another curious phenomenon. I have talked to other salespeople about it and found it was not unique with me. I told you about the end-of-the-day cold call. Sometimes there wasn't one in that trip area. Nevertheless, if I chased away the inner voice that was saying, "You've done enough for today; it's time to go home," and made one more call it was more often than not the most productive visit of the day. Why? I think it is for the same reasons that the day-end cold calls are good. At the time I didn't analyze it, but I have seen it often enough to be convinced of its validity.

If you make one more call a day, it amounts to about two hundred thirty more calls a year. That's enough to make a difference. That's enough to raise your income.

In his book, *How I Raised Myself From Failure To Success In Selling,* Frank Bettger quotes from a short talk the chairman of a life insurance company was making to a group of sales representatives. The chairman said this: "... after all, this business of selling narrows down to one thing -- just one thing, seeing the people. Show me any person of ordinary ability who will go out and earnestly tell his story to four or five people every day and I'll show you a person who just can't help making good."

I do not endorse sales representatives who make lots of calls for the sole purpose of building call numbers. I've known a few like that. However, I do applaud those who strive to maximize the time in front of customers and prospects with high quality calls.

If you make no contacts, you will sell nothing. If you make a lot of contacts, you could sell a lot.

The Telephone Can Increase Your Contacts

While traveling in my territory one day, Gordon and I were discussing the value of the telephone in selling. He recounted that for a few years, he was selling a product to feed manufacturers. He joined the Chicago Feed Club, a group that met monthly for dinner. One night a feed grains salesman, a casual acquaintance, approached Gordon during the reception and asked, "Do you know Bob Griffiths? If he's here, please point him out to me."

"Sure, I know Bob. You don't?," Gordon replied. Griffiths was purchasing agent for one of the country's largest feed manufacturers.

"Oh, I know him," the salesman said, " I've been selling him feed grains for four years, but I've never <u>seen</u> him. All our dealings have been on the telephone."

Griffiths' office and the salesman's office were both in Downtown Chicago, four blocks apart. In the salesman's defense, it was common in his business to sell by phone. However, it seemed strange that he could do business with someone so close for four years and never go see him.

My point is one often overlooked by sales representatives who normally see their customers and prospects face-to-face: You don't have to <u>see</u> people to sell them. People buy over the telephone. They also buy from letters, flyers and catalogues.

Can you combine face-to-face selling with the telephone and increase your coverage and your sales? Yes, you can.

Solve A Problem

When I was a sales manager, Gail, one of the sales

representatives, had a problem with one of her customers she visited once every month. The problem was that the buyer wouldn't turn down incoming telephone calls when she was in his office trying to get an order. The result was that Gail couldn't get across a coherent story because of repeated interruptions.

Furthermore, Gail could tell from listening to the buyer that these calls were almost always from sales representatives. More often than not they were getting agreement on an order or a shipping date. So, here was Gail, trying to get business on a face-to-face contact while competitive sales representatives were being given priority over the telephone.

Gail wisely decided to join the game. She dropped her personal visits from once a month to twice a year and used the telephone the other months. The face-to-face calls had been consuming two to four hours, including driving time. Now she was completing calls in fifteen to twenty minutes and with improved results.

What was the buyer's reaction to substituting telephone calls for personal visits? Curiously, he had no reaction at all -- he never mentioned it. A personal visit takes more of the buyer's time than a telephone call. Chances are he would prefer to use that time for other work, just as it pleased Gail to recover the time she had been spending on these personal visits. However, a buyer will seldom say to a sales representative, "Why don't you give me a phone call instead of coming in?"

Forward Thinking Is A Key

In the crop protection business we conducted technical information meetings for farmers during late fall and winter months between harvest and planting. The meetings were usually cosponsored by a local retail farm supply dealership. Once I was traveling with a salesperson for two days in early fall. The only objective for those two days was to set dates with each dealer for the farmer meetings. We accomplished the mission.

At the conclusion of the two days I congratulated the salesperson on his ability to get the cooperation of each dealer in setting mutually agreeable meeting dates.

Then I asked him if he thought it was necessary to see each dealer in person to make those dates. After all, he had called on them for several years and knew them well. Could he not have just picked up the telephone and accomplished in one-half day what had taken us two days, not to mention the expense and exposure of driving?

His answer was straight forward, "I don't know. It just never occurred to me not to drive."

I was thinking about this on the trip back to my office. We provide our sales representatives with a vehicle to get to customers and visual aids for explanation and demonstration. We ask them to file itineraries of their trips and we give them forms to record the visits and other forms to record the number of calls and mileage each day. In sales meetings we talk about efficient route planning. All of this is geared either directly or by implication toward being out seeing customers and prospects face-to-face.

Why should it surprise me that our sales representatives think they are drivers and visitors and don't think of the telephone as a major selling tool?

Ask a salesperson what he does and he'll reply, "I cover the Mid-Atlantic States for ABC Company." He thinks about personal, physical coverage of a given piece of geography.

Typically, salespeople will lay out a trip plan for a day or a week and then ask themselves, "What do I want to accomplish with each customer along the route?"

Wouldn't it make more sense to first look at each customer's file and ask yourself what you want to accomplish with this customer this week? Then you ask one more question, "Can I do it as effectively over the telephone or do I really need to see the customer?"

Some sellers might react to that suggestion by saying, "But, I'm going to drive right by that customer to get to others. Isn't it better to stop in?" The answer is: no, it is not. It will take time to stop -- yours and the customer's time. If you can accomplish what you want to do as effectively over the telephone, use the phone. You will pick up time for additional calls and additional calls bring in more income.

Plan Your Telephone Calls

You will accomplish more over the telephone if you follow a simple procedure:

- Jot down the subjects you want to cover during the call.
- Ask the buyer if he has the time to talk to you.
- Tell the buyer the number of items you want to discuss.

If you put the same forethought into a telephone call that you put into a face-to-face sales call, you will get a more satisfying result.

Writing down the points you want to cover during the

call is important. At the end of the conversation you won't have to say, "There is one more item I wanted to take up with you and now it has slipped my mind." A statement like that doesn't sound well on the other end of the line, not to mention that it will require another call when you do remember the item.

Few people can resist the ring of the telephone. However, that doesn't mean they are not in the middle of a piece of work or a conversation with an associate. Even if you are making a social call it is polite to start with, "Do you have time to talk with me now?"

You should not assume the buyer is ready to talk to you just because he picked up the phone. Furthermore, if you are going to get done what you want to accomplish on this call, you have to get the buyer's agreement to listen and talk. Ask for it. You can say, "I have three items this morning and it will take about ten minutes. Can you take the time now?"

If the buyer gives you a negative reply, you, of course, ask for a more convenient time and you call back then. It is always more fruitful to talk to at a time agreeable to the buyer.

By telling the buyer the number of items you wish to discuss you eliminate the possibility of being cut off or tuned out before you have covered all your items. You have piqued his curiosity and prepared him to stay with you until the end.

Qualifying The Prospect

The telephone is an invaluable tool for qualifying prospective customers. You don't have to see a buyer to know if his business and your product have a chance of fitting. You can find out eighty percent of what you want to know without taking the time to drive around in your car.

Start with telephone receptionists, whom you treat with the greatest respect. Ask what their company does. Most likely, you'll learn the names of the president, sales manager, and other key people. Many sellers don't try to have a conversation with telephone receptionists -- they're just hurrying through this conversation to reach somebody else. If receptionists have the time, they'll be glad to talk to you. If they don't have the time, ask for transfer to one of the administrative assistants.

Another source of information is the salespeople of your prospect. Not many sellers call the sales department for information, so your inquiry, out of the normal run of phone calls, will grab their attention. You and the salespeople of your prospect are both part of the same profession. Tell them what you need to know and why. They'll be understanding and will often give you a great deal of valuable information.

Even before you start gathering qualifying information over the telephone visit the reference section of your local library. There you will find books giving detailed information on most companies -- products, services, organizational structure, names, addresses, and telephone numbers of key people. If you are selling to people outside the manufacturing arena such as municipalities, financial institutions, associations, or almost anybody, you'll find information on them in your library, too. Even a small library has these books.

And, of course, the Internet is a powerful tool. With the click of a mouse, you can have a huge amount of valuable information at your fingertips.

Telephoning For Appointments

It is better to telephone in advance of a face-to-face contact than not to -- that's a good rule. However, as in all rules, there are exceptions. If the customer expresses a preference for you to visit without an appointment, of course, you do it. If you are selling a one-time item and the prospects are all lined up in a row, making appointments may be more time consuming than it's worth.

How far in advance should you make appointments? It depends entirely on the circumstances. If you know the customer will have several people to meet with you, a minimum of one week in advance is advisable -- it could be more. The customer may need time to gather information before your meeting or to schedule a conference room. Some types of sales demonstrations -- such as for heavy road building equipment -- require the buyer, along with others in the company, to join you in the field. You can't schedule that at the last minute.

If it is a one-on-one sales call, a day or two in advance may be enough. In some circumstances, you may even wish to telephone in the morning for an afternoon visit or as little as an hour before your arrival. Most buyers resent salespeople thinking they can drop in anytime with no prior consent.

When you have made an appointment a week or more in advance, it is usually a good idea to reconfirm the date and time the day before the appointment.

Why should you make appointments? There are several reasons:

1. *Courtesy.* It is good manners not to presume on the customer's time and availability. Do you really

like to have people drop in on you unannounced? Do you want to start a selling interview with the customer thinking, "I wish this person wasn't here"?

2. *Importance.* It lends importance to your sales call. A customer or prospect will think, "If this seller's time is too valuable to waste on useless calls, he must have something worth hearing." Because the customer considers your call important, he'll be a more attentive listener.

3. *Preparation.* It is smart to telephone for appointments because it gives customers time to prepare for the business discussion -- time to do their homework just as you have time to do yours. This works in your favor. Any sales representative would prefer talking to a prospect who knows in advance the area of discussion and has prepared for it. There's not much point in talking about facial tissues when the buyer thinks the subject is corrugated boxes.

4. *Time-savings.* The typical travel pattern for many sales people is often somewhat of a zig-zag route. If the day begins in City A and finishes in Town B, it is unlikely all the calls are on the main thoroughfare between the two locations. The route zig-zags to the right and left of the most direct route. City A and Town B may be only 50 miles apart, but route of travel might extend 150 miles or more in getting from one to the other.

As a sales manager traveling with salespeople, I found the practice of making side trips without reconfirming appointments was common. It was almost as though the sales representatives perceived their job as that of driving a car from customer to customer rather than that of making productive use of time to build the business.

Here's a typical example during a travel day with Brad. He was hired directly from college and had been in the territory about six months. We arrived at a customer's office just a couple of minutes before noon. Brad jumped out of the car, rushed into the building and was back in the car in less than a minute.

Brad: That makes me mad.

Chuck: Were you stood up?

Brad: I sure was. The guy went to lunch. It isn't even noon yet.

Chuck: What time was your appointment?

Brad: Eleven-thirty. But you saw how Taylor held us up on the last call. It wasn't possible to get here sooner.

Chuck: I understand, but couldn't you have phoned ahead as we left?

Brad: How did I know this guy was going to leave for lunch?

Chuck: Well . . . you didn't. But if you had called when we left Taylor's, you could have been sure he didn't go to lunch. Better yet, he might have joined us. That way we could have made very productive use of this next hour.

Brad: Frankly, it never occurred to me. I'm sorry. We may as well go get some lunch ourselves. They said he would be back by one-thirty. Now the schedule for the rest of the day is all messed up.

I checked Brad's reports over the next couple of months and noted that his phone bills went up, but so did his contacts. He learned quickly.

On another occasion I was traveling with a sales representative when we took a fifteen mile side trip to pick up an extra call. It turned out the customer was on vacation. By the time we got to the following customer, where we had an appointment, we were thirty minutes late and the customer had left ten minutes before we got there. So, we lost two calls. The first one we would have lost anyway because he was on vacation, but we could have found that out with the telephone and made the second call on time. Also, we could have called from the side-trip town and told the second customer we were on the way.

With cellular telephones standard equipment for many sales representatives today, calling requires little time and effort.

5. *Productivity.* This is really a summation of the first four reasons. Telephoning in advance for an appointment, whether it's a month, a week, a day or only an hour, assures you of a higher percent of productive contacts. As successful salespersons know, the easiest and most direct way to make your income grow is to increase the ratio of orders to calls and make more calls.

About a year after the incident with the fifteen mile side trip that resulted in no contact and made us miss an appointment, Tony, the salesperson, was in the office and we were having a cup of coffee together. The conversation went like this:

Tony: Chuck, do you remember the day we spent together and I took that fifteen mile side trip only to find the person was on vacation?

Chuck: I remember it. However, you had good intentions. You thought you could pick up an extra call over the noon hour.

Tony: Yes, that's right, but it wasn't smart. I took your advice and ever since I've been using the telephone extensively.

Chuck: And since then you haven't called on one customer who was on vacation, right?

Tony: That's for sure. But, what I want to tell you is I've discovered more reasons for using the telephone than simply making and confirming appointments. I use it between face-to-face calls with many of my regular customers to cover various items that I don't really have to see them to accomplish.

Chuck: Good for you.

Tony: And, I use it as a preliminary sales call device with new prospects. It helps me screen out those who really aren't going to become customers. I save a lot of time I used to waste on non-productive personal visits. In all, the number of face-to-face calls has gone down while the total contacts has jumped dramatically, because of the telephone. My sales volume reflects the results.

Chuck: Yes it does and I'm more than pleased.

Writing Customers

Some sales representatives think of themselves solely as oral communicators and overlook the value of the written word. However, there are opportunities to write customers and prospects and thereby increase your coverage, or your effectiveness, or both.

Here are three:

1. You can follow up a face-to-face sales call with a letter. A letter is especially useful if the sales call was complex. If you covered several topics during the visit, the chances of inaccurate or incomplete recall by the buyer are relatively high. Restating your points in writing will thwart that. I never met a buyer who didn't appreciate a summary letter, even when the call was not complex -- often they will comment about it on your next visit. If your call frequency is low, a follow-up letter has the effect of stretching one visit into two. If you write nothing more than, "I know you were busy Monday so I'm doubly grateful you took the time to see me," it will, at least, give the customer another reason to think of you favorably. Of course, you may wish to add more such as thanks for the order or ask again, if you didn't get an order.

2. Some sales representatives make good use of periodic mass-produced letters that offer helpful information or carry a direct selling message or do

both. Though the buyer may not regard such a letter as highly as a personal letter, these letters do keep your name before the buyer and span the gap between personal visits.

When I moved to my first sales territory, my regional office sent a letter and brochure to customers and prospects announcing my presence in the territory. The brochure included a photo and a brief biographical sketch. With the letter, buyers knew I was ready to help them, and they had my address and telephone number. One day when calling on a dealership for the first time the manager greeted me, "Chuck, I've been expecting you." The brochure was even tacked to the bulletin board. How does that compare to your first call on a customer?

3. A short, long-hand note can often accomplish as much as a longer, more formal letter. Suppose you just received a supply of literature on your company's new product. You could put it in your sales literature file for distribution to your customers as you call on them. You also could clip a long-hand note to the literature saying, "Please look at this and we'll discuss it when we get together," and mail it to all your customers and prospects. Some sales representatives have note pads with their name, address, phone, fax, and e-mail address printed on them for this and other informal uses.

In spite of appointments, customers occasionally will disappoint you and not be available for your meeting. Perhaps the buyer forgot or some last minute emergency arose. The usual response is to hand your calling card to the receptionist while saying, "Please tell Mr. Buyer I was here."

The card and the message certainly do the job of letting the buyer know you kept the appointment. However, there is also an implicit rebuke in the blunt statement and the cold card.

Can you convert a no-interview call into something positive? Yes, you can. You can take a sheet of note paper, such as the one suggested above, and write a note to leave behind. You might write, "Sorry to have missed you today. I'll see you again in two weeks. The matter can wait until then."

Whether or not you had an appointment, if you can't get in to see the buyer, you can clip a note to a piece of literature and leave it with the receptionist. "Here is literature about our new product. I'd like to discuss it with you in person and will call you Friday for an appointment next week. There is much more than this brochure shows, but, at least, it is a start. Sorry I missed you this time."

If you are making a cold call and can't get time with the buyer, your note might read, "I took a chance by stopping in today. I appreciate your frankness in telling me you were busy because it does take thirty minutes to explain the advantages of our new system -- advantages that can earn extra money for you. I'll call you tomorrow at 10 o'clock to make an appointment for a more suitable time."

You have many opportunities in selling to supplement and complement personal visits with notes and letters. Short notes may even be best -- they take less of your time to write and less of your customer's time to read.

The More You Contact The More You Sell

I've talked about techniques for making as many contacts as possible without sacrificing the quality of your sales calls. You can do it in several ways:

- Time your visits to suit the customers. They'll be more receptive and you'll accomplish more.
- Plan your travel routes for efficiency. You'll read more about this in the next chapter.
- Use the telephone.
- Write letters and notes.

Now, it is in your hands. Start with just one action with one customer. It will grow from there.

Chapter V

Organization

"Good order is the foundation of all good things."
Edmund Burke, 1729-1797

Summary: Every well-organized salesperson is not a top seller, but every top seller is a well-organized salesperson. In computer terms, this is the salesperson's operating system.

Introduction

The attributes discussed in the first four chapters of this book account for a seller's success. However, to capitalize on those attributes to the fullest you have to add one more -- organization.

Salespeople often neglect organization. They may exhibit the other four attributes, but are held back from reaching their full potential because of lack of organization. They have a gummed-up operating system. Organization of selling activities and selling tools is the weak link.

Most sales representatives agree that efficient organization will make their work easier, multiply their time and effectiveness in front of customers and result in greater sales and higher income. The problem is not recognition of the need and the benefits, rather it is the lack of know-how. They don't know how to build and use files, how to gather records and analyze them and how to develop work-efficient schedules. They don't know the tools nor how to use them.

Computers or Paper

When I started my selling career, salespeople weren't using computers. It is a very different situation today. However, whether you use computers or pencils and paper makes no difference -- the same processes apply. As you read this section, picture the files and forms on a computer screen or on paper. They'll work to your advantage either way.

In time, a salesperson may develop a workable, organized system independently, with no outside help. I've known a few such people. However, if someone introduces you to sound rules of organization and you follow them, you will reach a high level of performance more rapidly than by the trials and errors of the self-taught route.

The information in this chapter is valuable for both the veteran and the beginning salesperson. Either one is an eager student of something that promises an increase in sales and income.

Why Organize For Selling?

Aside from the ultimate purpose of selling more goods and services and earning more money, several immediate benefits of organizing for better selling surface.

When you are organized you have more time and attention to devote to income-producing activities. Why is that? Because you have been wasting time shuffling papers and looking for information you can't find. Once you establish efficient routines to support your selling function, more time is available for selling.

The alternative to good organization is a future handicapped by wasteful periods of hasty planning and preparation and frantic searching and shuffling before your sales calls, and even then not having everything you need.

In the following pages I will discuss the advantages of efficient filing and show you ways to set up a simple, useful system -- classifications, titles, folders, containers, location and, above all, profitable use and control of the system.

I'll also discuss how to deal with screening and handling the endless flow of paper, how to plan and complete your day, and how to plan your call routing.

Files For Salespeople On The Go

Paperwork is to selling what wheels are to an automobile. Though wheels are not the driving force, your car cannot move forward without them. Instead of futilely ranting at the paper, let's see if you can manipulate it to your benefit.

Turning this unavoidable paper pile to your advantage begins with organized files -- they are the foundation of any paperwork system. The job is not formidable. I'm not talking about a bank of file cabinets. I'm talking about a few files tailored to the size and scope of your selling activities.

A salesperson's files could be as simple as one or two indexed loose-leaf binders. Or, they may be file folders split up among several small portable file boxes. Or, they may be diskettes that you slip into your computer. Or, they may be a combination of these systems. The emphasis is not on storage of information, but on use of information. A sales representative's files are working tools.

The busiest seller can set up the simple, but complete filing system I will outline with a minimum tax on his or her time.

Office procedures experts or salespeople with a penchant for extreme detail, after reading the following pages, might say, "But, I could design a far better, more complete filing system than that."

They could, and so could I. But, it's not necessary. Sales representatives do not need extensive files unless they want to spend endless hours setting up an elaborate system of minutely classified and sub-classified papers and more endless hours maintaining it. Filing is not the goal. Selling -- better selling -- is the goal.

This filing system provides a place for you to put every bit of information as soon as you lay your hands on it. The aim of the system is to ensure you have all the information available when and where you need it and reduce to an absolute minimum the time you spend handling the information.

Before taking up specific files, it might be helpful to consider a few basic ideas.

File Purpose

The purpose of a file is to classify, index and store information so you can readily retrieve it. A file is like an encyclopedia -- with one big difference. In an encyclopedia finding information is a delayed process. The reader must first look up the title in the index. The index remotely leads you to the subject on a choice of pages. From that it leads you through cross-references to additional sections of the encyclopedia.

On the other hand, a file instantly locates the information. The title and the subject are in the same place -- in a precisely indexed folder, loose-leaf binder, or diskette.

File Titles

In setting up a new file or in filing new material your choice of titles is very important. Keep in mind the primary aim of ready retrieval. Pick titles that will mean the same to you a few months from now that they mean today.

If you are filing a bulletin from headquarters on automobile safety, how would you title the file? Would you write, "Bulletins from Home Office?" Or, "Automobile Safety?" Or, "Safety, Automobiles?" Or, "Driving Safety?" Without question you can discard the first title -- it is too all-inclusive for ready retrieval. The next three titles are all acceptable. If every time you think of the subject the word "automobile" comes to mind, "Automobile Safety" is the title for your file. However, if "automobile" is not always your primary thought association, and "Safety" or "Driving" is as likely to pop into your head, you may need to put a cross-reference in your file. Remember: ready retrieval is your goal.

Whatever form of file you are using -- I'll discuss several later -- always keep blanks available so you can easily make up new titles as you receive new material. If you are using a paper system, this stock will include the whole paraphernalia -- blank folders, dividers, and tabs.

A common error is to under-classify, to settle on a few general titles and sort and store information accordingly.

"Bulletins from Home Office," as in the example above, is just such a general, but not very useful file.

The encyclopedia index, with sub-classifications under many of the titles, could be a guide for you to follow. Of course, you might over-classify. However, familiarity with your job and the need for support by file-stored information will act as a brake on any tendency towards file subdivisions beyond reason.

File Size

Keep files pared down to practical size. The thicker the file on a subject, the less useful it is. If it takes more than a few seconds to locate the information you need, that particular subject grouping needs revision. You can solve the problem in either one or both of these two ways:

1. Throw away part of the file. It is highly probable the file contains information no longer useful. Cull outdated material so you won't be carrying useless paper and, what's more important, won't be distributing out-of-date information.
2. A thick file may be a sign of under-classification. The subject should be further broken down under additional subtitles. The few minutes you spend on this chore will pay off by ending future loss of time in extensive searches for information. Salespeople must keep their files alive -- retain the items needed and, without hesitation, get rid of those not needed.

There will be times when you can't be sure if a piece of information is worth saving or not. Probably, you will file it under its proper title. If the information lies undisturbed for a whole year, discard it -- you didn't need it in the first place. It is just clutter in your tool box.

Here is a six-point summary of the basic rules for a sales representative's files:

1. A file is an active tool.
2. Ready retrieval is your primary goal.
3. Choose titles you can remember.
4. Write new titles liberally -- do not under-classify.
5. Keep your files thin.
6. Discard information you don't use or that is out-of-date.

Six Files For Sales Representatives

A salesperson requires six major file classifications for territory administration and operation. Everything needed and everything received can be put into one of these six file groupings:

1. Administrative
2. Competitive
3. Market Data
4. Technical
5. Sales Literature
6. Customers and Prospects

These are six classifications, not just six file folders nor six computer files. All the classifications or file groupings have subdivisions. The subdivisions will vary from file to file and salesperson to salesperson. In one case it might require a file box of many subdivisions -- separate folders or sections each containing a subject that falls within one of the six major classifications. Or, in another case, you can house the entire file in one loose-leaf binder, subdivided by tab sheets. In every case the principles outlined above -- about titling for ready retrieval, thickness of files and discarding useless information -- constantly apply.

In the next six sections I'll talk about each of these file groupings with particular attention to their contents and use.

Administrative File

This file contains those items a salesperson needs to work the territory. The titles of the other five files are specific. Therefore, you could define the Administrative File as containing all those items not obviously falling into one of the other five file categories. Here are some of the items:

Blank forms
Credit guides
Expense reports
Hotel directories
Job description
Mailing lists
Company organization chart
Maps
Safety bulletins
Sales cost analysis
Sales forecasts and goals
Sales performance records
Sales training materials

This is one file group where you will often add new

titles, so be sure the folders, dividers, tabs or whatever it is you use are always available.

The Administrative File also should include a "tickler" or "bring-up" file divided into periods -- months, weeks and days. This is a convenient drop for items you purposely put off for action at a future specific date. The file provides for almost automatic retrieval on the date you want the action to take place. Of course, you do have to look in the tickler file each day (or each week, if you haven't broken it down to individual days).

Not every item for future action belongs in the tickler file. "Ask Customer A for dinner date on next visit," for example belongs in the customer file (we'll discuss it later). On the other hand, "Call Customer B on January 20 for a dinner date," belongs in the tickler file for that date.

The tickler file is a calendar with a built-in alarm clock. It is especially helpful in alerting you to periodic responsibilities such as writing a monthly report or quarterly sales forecasts. You will keep your sales manager happy as you always submit reports punctually -- and that won't hurt you a bit. It may even make you feel good.

Unless your job is of the utmost simplicity, an amply titled Administrative File is indispensable.

Competitive File

You should know as much about the strengths and weaknesses of competitive products as you do about your own. You keep that information in your Competitive File.

Multi-product salespersons might choose to classify all competitive information under company names. Or, they might find an advantage in a two-way classification, first by product type and then company name.

In any case, the competitive literature should be available for use on sales calls. If the customer raises the subject of product comparison, you can contrast the relevant features of your product with the competitive product.

In such a situation reference to the competitor's own printed literature (or even the actual product) will bring you several benefits. It will:

1. Enhance your image. "This salesperson deals in facts and knows what he is talking about," the customer will think to himself.
2. Prevent misstatements about a competitive product that could later prove embarrassing.
3. Add visual reinforcement to your words.
4. Provide direct comparison that can give the sales call decided momentum in your direction.
5. Subtly increase the value of your proposal for the business by showing you are confident and not afraid of comparison.
6. Give you the valuable opportunity to guide the comparison that the customer would otherwise make alone.

The advantages of using a competitor's literature as a selling aid for your own product suggest you may wish to ask if the prospect would welcome direct comparison. Asking this question calls for assertiveness and statements that adroitly and tactfully lead the buyer into inviting the comparison.

This suggestion might run counter to your practice. However, it is not the senseless tactic of knocking a competitor. This approach yields a dispassionate balancing of fact against fact <u>after</u> the customer signifies interest in a comparison. It is not a gratuitous introduction of the competitor's name to disparage his product.

When you have skillfully probed the buyer's attitude, if he gives no indication that product comparisons are on his mind, drop the subject. However, if he does invite comparison, have at it. Use the competitor's own literature to help the buyer make a fair and factual comparison.

An orderly Competitive File, providing for ready retrieval of competitive literature for use on sales calls, is a valuable tool for the ambitious sales representative.

Market Data File

If you have no part in setting your own territory goals, you may not need a Market Data File. On the other hand, if your job permits you to exercise discretion in any of the following areas, you do need a Market Data File:

- Size of territory
- Geographical emphasis within the territory
- Market emphasis within the territory
- Sales goals
- Advertising
- Sales promotion activity
- Allocation and direction of personal selling time
- Planning future needs and action

The Market Data File contains useful facts about the market or markets within your territory. These data help you plan and direct the responsibilities listed above.

The nature and needs of your markets will determine

the data sources. They could include such suppliers of market information as:

- Banks
- Chambers of Commerce
- State Government Departments
- Federal Government Departments (Agriculture, Commerce, etc.)
- Surveys of Buying Power by *Sales & Marketing Management* magazine
- Surveys by market specialists
- Surveys by the trade and business press
- Surveys by your company
- Surveys by you

If you sell through retail or wholesale distributors, your Market Data File can do double duty. From this file you can pass on information that will enable them to do a better job of selling your product.

The justification of the Market Data File, as with all the files, is utility. If it is solely a collection of statistics that offer no guidance, it is worthless.

If a salesperson is selling supplies to retail bakeries in an assigned geographic area, has no competition and can't change territory boundaries, is there need to collect and analyze market data? Probably not.

However, change just one of those assumptions and you can see how a market data file can be a valuable tool. If the salesperson has the authority to alter the territory, or, at least, is free to discuss possible changes with management, there are several data necessary for assembling a compelling case:

- Number of retail bakeries
- Location of those bakeries
- Dollar purchases of each bakery
- Total dollar purchases of his territory

For simplification, let's assume the profit for the salesperson and the company does not vary by product or store location. Analysis of the four facts above might lead to any number of conclusions. Here are some possibilities:

- Total dollars won't support one salesperson
- Total dollars are more than one salesperson can service
- Dollar purchases of some bakeries are too small to justify sales calls
- Dollar purchases of some bakeries justify more attention than available time allows
- Number of bakeries are too numerous to visit with even a minimum call schedule
- Location of some bakeries argues against covering them at all when the cost of travel and time are laid along side their dollar purchases

Each of these findings, alone or in combination with others, could lead to a beneficial change in the territory boundaries or emphasis within an assigned territory.

Let's take a second example, this time based on the assumption the sales representative does have competition. Here are some of the market data to develop, plus questions that logically flow from these data.

Total dollar purchases of the territory

What is my company's share? How much does

each competitor have?

Territory purchases by product

Do I have the right products?

Seasonal variations of product purchases

Do I have the products needed? Do I anticipate seasonal changes and time my selling to correspond?

Product preferences from one area to another

Do I have a broad enough line? Am I flexible enough to sell the products that fit?

Location and dollar purchases of each bakery

Travel time and costs considered, what is the potential profit from each bakery? Am I allocating my time in proportion to business potential? Could I profitably abandon some small bakeries and spend more time with large ones?

You could carry on the analysis through the introduction of other relevant factors toward the perfection of marketing strategy.

The Market Data File should lead you to set sales and profit goals that challenge to your capabilities.

Markets are constantly changing and you must keep the file abreast of the changes by adding new data as you come across them and removing old data no longer pertinent.

Not all companies have market research groups to feed data to their sales representatives. However, that in no way lessens the need for such data. What it does do is place the job on the shoulders of the individual salespeople. Their shoulders may be a good place for it anyway. Sellers who collect and interpret their own data will be more agreeable to changing their course to meet the sales and profit goals.

One common fault of sales representatives is to assume their job is to cover a given piece of geography. It would be more to the point to define the job as a responsibility to sell a certain amount of goods and return an assigned profit. I have heard sales managers tell their salespeople: "Once you and I agree on your sales goal, I could care less where you sell it. If you can move the entire quantity in one county and ignore the other counties, that's all right with me. Your primary job is to make the goal, not to cover geography."

The countless salespeople who view their job as something more purposeful than driving around an assigned piece of the country are the creative salespeople and the ones who sell the most. You can be sure the Market Data File stands out with them as an indispensable planning tool.

Technical File

Sometimes all the facts salespeople need to support their selling positions are in their give-away literature. More frequently, however, this is not the case. For brevity, or fear that too much detail might be a turn-off, interesting facts about the product are omitted from sales literature.

These left-out facts, while of little immediate interest to the customer or prospect, can be of untold benefit to the salesperson. They deepen product knowledge, bolster self-assurance in the give-and-take with customers, and lend support toward achieving the sale.

The technical file will contain items such as these:

- Product bulletins from product managers or engineering staff

- Letters an engineer may have written to customers that contain information you know you can use with other customers
- Reprints of articles about the specific product or about the type of product
- Research reports from your company or an outside agency
- Any information contributing to depth of knowledge about the product -- information you can use to support selling arguments, answer questions or overcome objections.

What distinguishes the Technical File from the Sales Literature File is this: the Technical File contains information not produced for general circulation or not now in general circulation. It includes out-of-print material and material gathered from various sources such as technical journals. In essence, the Technical File is an encyclopedia for a particular product or group of associated products.

You must jealously guard the contents of your Technical File. Never give away one of the documents -- it may be irreplaceable. Besides that, you may need it on the very next call the same day.

Some sales representatives think it reflects negatively on their competence to refer to their Technical File in front of the customer. I disagree. Customers don't expect sales representatives to carry everything in their head. It would be a waste of time -- not to mention next to an impossibility -- to memorize myriad technical details, some of which you may need only occasionally. Indeed, the answer to a buyer's query is more authoritative if you support it with a reference from your Technical File.

You should be so thoroughly familiar with your Technical File that you can retrieve any document without rummaging. Later I'll discuss the use of the Technical File in preparation for a day's work in calling on customers and prospects.

Technical knowledge was the first attribute discussed at the beginning of this book. Intimate knowledge of your product, its capabilities, features, and the benefits it offers customers is, indeed, a paramount attribute. Your Technical File is the repository of that information.

Sales Literature File

The Sales Literature File is your give-away file. It holds product literature, sales promotion material, advertising reprints and other printed and audio/video sales aids to leave with or mail to customers.

In advance of your sales call select the literature you expect to leave with the customer. Limit yourself, if possible, to the single most informative piece for that particular customer. It should be the one that best supports or illustrates the product or service benefits you want to emphasize. The selection may vary from customer to customer or from visit to visit.

It is not uncommon to have three or four different pieces of literature on the same product, but it is seldom wise to leave all of them with the customer or prospect. The array may confuse the buyer and defeat the purpose of the literature. The purpose is to reinforce your proposal or serve as reference when you are not in the buyer's presence.

Another suggestion is to underline or highlight those sections of the literature you particularly want the buyer to read. It adds emphasis to your proposal to mark the material in the buyer's office with him looking on. However, if that is not practical, mark it in advance. One way or another be sure to mark it.

Did you ever try to read something while another person is talking to you? What is the result? You don't understand what you're reading and you don't comprehend what the other person is saying. It is next to impossible to absorb anything in that situation. Buyers have no more ability in that regard than you. When you hand the customer a piece of literature to read, hand it to him with the print toward him and then be silent and let him read it.

Sales literature is money in your pocket, if you recognize how effective it can be. Keep it clean, up-to-date, and use it intelligently.

Customer and Prospect File

This sixth and last file grouping, as the title reads, holds information on customers and prospective customers. You should have a computer file on each or, if you are using a paper system, a file folder on each. What should go into the file?

Customer Data Sheet

The first item in the folder or computer file is the Customer Data Sheet. It contains basic information -- correct company name and full address, zip code, telephone and fax numbers and electronic mail address. It also holds the correct name of company personnel -- the top officers plus others you may contact. And, lastly, you will put there other information of a permanent or semi-permanent nature that will help you establish and maintain a profitable relationship with your customer.

The Customer Data Sheet is the most valuable and most referred to document in your files. For better understanding between the two of us, let's expand a bit on the information recorded there.

Correct Name and Full Address

Why do I say, "Correct name and full address?" Why not just the name and address? It is because owners chose their company name after much thought. They are proud of it and it doesn't make them happy to see it abbreviated or misspelled. If the company name is, "Agency Distribution Company, Ltd.," please don't write, "Agency Dist. Co.," when addressing an envelope to them.

It is the same with personal names. If your name were James C. Davies how would you react to a letter addressed to Mr. Jim Davies or to Mr. C. J. Davies? Maybe it wouldn't bother you, but there are those among your customers whom it could irritate, especially if the shortening involved uninvited use of a nickname. It is not a great big matter. However, why risk introducing even a minor irritation when you know nobody objects to seeing their name printed in full and correctly?

When you see your customer, James C. Davies, in person, what do you call him? James? Jim? or Mr. Davies? Does it make a difference? Not always, but it does sometimes.

To illustrate the importance of a person's name, my mentor, Gordon, told me about a customer who bought tank carloads of ammoniating solutions for his fertilizer plants. When Gordon first moved to the territory he had none of this customer's business. However, after a few months he began to get a tank car now and then and, by the time two years had passed, it seemed he had all, or almost all, of the business. What had accounted for this substantial turnaround?

Gordon recalled the general manager and buyer was Walter Brown. He was in his late fifties or early sixties and Gordon was about thirty. Brown always wore a well-tailored suit, a starched white shirt, and a conservative necktie. His office was spacious, carpeted, and expensively furnished.

When he first called at this business, Gordon was struck by Mr. Brown's formality, so he addressed him as Mr. Brown. Gordon was never invited to call him any other name and, given the difference in ages, he always felt comfortable calling him Mr. Brown. In fact, Gordon never used his first name, not with him nor in talking with anyone else in his company.

"On the other hand" Gordon recalled, "when I attended meetings where he was present, I noticed all my competitors' salespeople calling him Walter, Wally, or Walt. In a way it seemed silly that one small thing like that could make the difference in buying behavior, but to this day I can't pin it on anything else."

You will not irritate a man by calling him Mr. nor a woman by calling her Ms. Indeed, if your customers come from societies of formality, such as in most European countries, they bristle at your attempts at informality. If a person prefers to be addressed other than as Mr. or Ms., either they'll tell you or you'll pick it up indirectly. Find out how your customer likes to be addressed and make a note next to his or her name on your Customer Data Sheet.

Titles

Record the title of each person you contact. It tells you where he or she fits into the organization and indicates the level of responsibility. However, titles do not always tell the whole story. The meaning of titles may vary from company to company. In some businesses, several Divisions comprise a Department and in others it is the reverse. In one company General Managers are top executives with several Directors reporting to them. In another company General Managers are in a lower echelon with Directors above them.

Know the titles and visualize the interrelationships existing within the buyer's organization. A good way to do this is to draw an organization chart. Find out the scope of responsibility at each level in the company.

Your purpose, of course, is to define the purchasing hierarchy -- who participates in the decision process, and who has the final word?

Personal Data

In the second chapter of this book I wrote about this same subject. It is worth repeating. Russ had what he called his People Card. An alternative and perhaps better place to record personal facts is on the Customer Data Sheet.

As you become better acquainted with people, their conversation will contain references to family, hobbies, and likes and dislikes. In the case of a customer or prospect, these bits of information are worth recording to serve as amenities in future stages of the flourishing relationship.

If you make notes of personal information right after leaving a person, it provides insurance against embarrassment in later contacts. You could even introduce a chill in customers' attitudes towards you by not remembering personal information they passed along to you.

Naturally, you can't rattle off everything customers tell you on previous visits without betraying that you are talking from a deliberately recorded transcript of their revelations. You have to bring the subject into the conversation smoothly, as an unlabored recollection. You must demonstrate that your sincerity in them resulted in your remembering personal details they were generous enough to share with you.

Unless you have a phenomenal memory, written notes are essential; your only safeguard against error in the recall of customer personal confidences.

Make a Record

There are three good reasons for writing or inputting information on your Customer Data Sheet instead of trying to keep it in your head.

1. A written record may be more accurate than your memory -- at least, less open to question.
2. Part of the information you garner from customers also transfers to your Market Data File -- each customer is part of your overall market.
3. You may be transferred and, if only for the customer's sake, your successor can pick up where you left off. The customer has every right to expect the new salesperson to fit into the relationship smoothly. Furthermore, fairness to your own company dictates that your replacement start his new assignment fully equipped with the information you gathered while in the territory. Otherwise, he will have to rebuild the Customer Data Sheet from scratch and use up time more profitably spent maintaining sales volume and sealing his contacts against competitive inroads.

Many salespeople write on the Customer Data Sheet a short summation of each call. It gives them a running record of their progress with the customer. These brief notes can substitute for call reports, unless your management demands one for each contact.

Paper or Computer

There will be frequent changes to make on your Customer Data Sheet. You may have additions, deletions and corrections to enter after each visit. Because of these changes, the sheet is ideally suited for a computer. Just pull up the current sheet on your screen and painlessly make the changes. Any number of computer "contact manager programs" will allow you to keep track of your customer data, provide an electronic reminder for upcoming events, word processing, and tracking sales.

However, if you are not using a computer, print your Customer Data Sheet on high-quality paper that can stand repeated use of an eraser. Enter your data in pencil and erase the data when you change it. You will be most comfortable when you know your Customer Data Sheets are always up-to-date.

Customer Sales Record Sheet

The second major division in each customer file is the Customer Sales Record Sheet. Outstanding salespeople keep their own record of customer purchases to guide their future dealings with each customer, set sales goals and measure their progress. Sales records are the yardstick by which they gauge success.

If you have instant access to sales history and current shipments through your computer, you may not need to keep a hand posted sheet. However, whether it is a computer printout or your own hand posted sheet, your sales record on each customer should meet these four specifications:

1. It should show, as a minimum, a three-year history of purchases.
2. It should permit you to see, at a glance, the state of the customer's purchases -- one subject for discussion during the sales call.
3. It should be up-to-date -- as current as today.
4. It should be in a form you can show to the customer.

Why do you need sales records on each customer that meet all four of these specifications? A history of purchases over an extended period, broken down by months (in some businesses, weeks), is helpful in several ways:

1. You can spot trends and use them for your own gain. Is there a significant movement within an industry? Is your business growing? Should your company increase manufacturing capacity? Do you see a weakness in your customer's business? Is the customer's competitor capturing part of the business and, indirectly, taking away part of your business? In that case, you may want to make a customer out of that competitor. Is a rival of yours making off with your business? You need to know.
2. If there is nothing you can do about the trend, at least, the knowledge of it will be useful to your company in projecting financial, manufacturing and marketing needs.

3. Having the customer's purchasing pattern clearly laid out in front of you will permit you to correlate your face-to-face contacts and telephone calls with the buyer's buying cycles -- you will be there to receive the order when he or she is ready.

One more very important reason for keeping the Customer Sales Record Sheet up-to-date is this: A grave insult to buyers is not to know they just placed an order with your company. If you receive records of customer purchases monthly, they may be two weeks old before you get them and six weeks old before you get the next one. On the other hand, if you enter daily invoices on your Customer Sales Record Sheet, the oldest data is the time it takes the information to get from the order processing center to you.

Of course, if you have a computer and access to home office records, you may be able to check customer purchases just before making each call. That is the best situation. If customers placed an order with your company yesterday, they expect you to know it and thank them.

The Customer Sales Record Sheet should be neat. You may want to show it to the buyer to illustrate or underscore some point in your discussion.

Reports, Correspondence and Notes

If you write reports on each call, a copy of the most recent one will be in your file folder for that particular customer or in your computer file. If it contains vital information, transcribe the gist of it to the Customer Data Sheet and throw the report away when you write the next one. Avoid an accumulation of old reports. Old reports take up space as well as your time.

Customer service representatives, engineers, or other people in your company may have written your customer since your last visit. Copies of this correspondence should be in the customer file folder.

You may wish to place in the folder reminders of items to take up on the next call -- things that came to mind since your last visit. One good time to think about the agenda for the next call is just after having left the customer's office. At that moment, his or her particular situation -- problems and opportunities -- are focused sharply and the course to follow on the next call may be more apparent now than later. Drop a note in the customer's folder for your next sales call.

Filing The Customer File Folders

You can arrange the files on all your customers and prospects in a file box or in your computer in alphabetical order, geographical order, or a mixture of the two.

If your territory is split into well-defined trip areas, you can file the customer folders alphabetically within each trip area. Then you might place a miscellaneous folder in the front of each trip area to drop in items not yet important enough for you to set up a separate file folder. You can review that folder each time you plan to enter the trip area. Ideally, it will be empty when you leave the area. You will either have disposed of the item or found it promising enough to set up a separate folder.

What is the order of importance of the six file groups? I wouldn't rank their importance as long as the Customer and Prospect File heads the list. Without customers there is no business, no territory, no need for sales representatives. Without accurate customer records there is no planned progress.

File Thirteen

While this file was not on the list you read earlier, in some respects, it is the most valuable file of all. It is the one file that permits you to keep all the others in useable shape. I don't know who coined the term "File Thirteen," but I like this euphemism for wastebasket. Freely used it is the prime factor in maintaining orderly, viable files. On your computer it is the "Delete" key.

At least fifty percent of all the paper you receive you can throw in File Thirteen. It is not because the information lacks interest, but because it doesn't have sufficient retention value to justify the time to file it and the space to hold it. Don't save information you have little chance of needing. It makes what you do need less accessible and less transportable.

Use File 13 generously. It is better to save a little too little than a little too much.

File Equipment

If all your files are on a computer, you can skip this section. However, even if you use a computer, you may have paper in your administrative file and in your sales literature file. This section assumes all the information you need is on paper. If that is not the case, you can ignore the parts that don't apply and adopt those that do.

What should you file your papers in? Individual file folders under the six file classifications? Or, should you use loose-leaf notebooks? Or, an alphabetized accordion file? Or, some other system?

All file systems have advantages and disadvantages. To some extent, how you use a particular file will dictate the choice. A mixture of equipment may be your answer.

Remember, a salesperson's files are not for storage, they are an operating system. In view of that, here are three objectives to keep in mind when choosing equipment:

- Easy to file papers
- Easy to retrieve papers
- Easy to use the system

It is unlikely one type of equipment will meet all three objectives equally. After you have related each type of equipment to the several file groupings -- bearing in mind the nature of the contents and the frequency and urgency of demand for the information -- one type of equipment will stand out as offering the easiest filing, retrieval and use for each file grouping.

For example, you might choose ring binders for some files. The one disadvantage is the relative difficulty of preparing paper for insertion. You have to punch holes in the paper, open the rings, insert the paper and close the rings. This is all time-consuming when you measure it against the simple act of dropping a paper into a file folder. A ring binder is not the ideal filing equipment when you must insert and withdraw papers frequently.

On the other hand, a ring binder has appealing advantages. The paper is in a relatively permanent place -- you can't easily lose it. The binder is convenient to use in your car or in the customer's office. You can file a large number of papers in one binder and, with divider sheets and tabs to provide the indexing, you can find quickly the paper you need.

A ring binder would meet your needs for the Market Data File, the Technical File and the Competitive File. These three files do not require frequent insertion or withdrawal of paper. The ring binder is the most convenient type of equipment when you have to refer to papers while you are with a customer.

You might wish to use more than one ring binder for a given file. If you sell several products, you might break down your Technical File into several binders. You can subdivide any file as much as you wish.

Choosing or rejecting file folders also is a matter of balancing advantages against disadvantages. File folders can be disorderly and papers can easily slip out when you handle them. But file folders allow more flexibility in titling and in arranging the order of titles quickly and easily. They also permit instant insertion and withdrawals -- it is easy to file papers and retrieve them.

File folders shape up as more adaptable to your needs for your Administrative File, your Sales Literature File, and your Customer and Prospect File.

Here are suggested equipment choices for the six file groups:

FILE	EQUIPMENT
Administrative	File Folders
Competitive	Ring Binders
Market Data	Ring Binders
Technical	Ring Binders
Sales Literature	File Folders or Boxes
Customer and Prospect	File Folders

File Location and File Containers

Your files are your working tools -- it is worth saying again. Where do you keep your tools? Except for most of your Administrative File, your files should be with you, ready to go to work for you every day at the moment you need them.

The one exception to this rule is the salesperson who is never away overnight and who knows at the end of each day what items from the files will be needed the following day. Those items are extracted from the files and placed in the briefcase for use the following day.

For other sales representatives the five files belong with you. When you take them with you the files are always available for sales calls and for the evening work in the hotel room.

The container for each file can be cardboard, wood, or metal. They should be slightly wider than a file folder or ring binder. Containers intended for use in a vehicle should be sized for safe and convenient access and for ease of handling in and out of the car or truck.

Handling Your Papers

I have never known a salesperson who didn't complain about paperwork. The seemingly endless flow of paper coming your way from company headquarters, customers, and sundry other sources tends to outrun your ability to decide about the merits of each piece and dispose of it promptly.

This simple system of six files -- plus File Thirteen -- prevents the pile-up of papers on your desk by giving you a place to put each piece of paper as soon as you read it. It gives you the machinery for making prompt judgments and disposition of all the papers you receive.

Let's see how it works.

You are ready to tackle the incoming mail and electronic messages.

At this point, many people sort their papers into several piles somewhat related to the final action they expect to take. After this preliminary sorting, they read each piece again and decide upon a course of action. Often this action is, "I'll put the paper in this other pile that I hope to get to someday." And, if that day ever comes, they then have to read it once again and, for the third time, decide.

The chief threat to efficient paper handling is procrastination -- the tendency to get mired in indecision. Indecision hobbles your productivity. It steals time from selling. It cheats you of income. It may even make you feel somewhat guilty. The offset to this threat is your own will power. Here is the formula to memorize and apply with determination:

READ   DECIDE   DO

If it requires action you can do immediately, do it.

If it requires action at a future, specific date, put it in the tickler file for that date.

If it concerns action with a particular customer on a future visit, put it in the customer's file folder.

If it is an order copy, post the data on the customer's sales record sheet and throw away the order copy.

If it is a call report you wish to keep until the next call, put it in the customer's file folder. If it contains no significant information, put it in File Thirteen.

If it is a newsletter or other information of no permanent value, store the information in your mind and put the paper in File Thirteen.

If it is technical information of permanent value, put it in the appropriate place in your technical file. If you can't guess how you would ever use that information, put the paper in File Thirteen.

If it is a new piece of sales literature, decide at once how many copies you want for your Sales Literature File and send in the order.

If it is some new market data, put it in your Market Data File.

If any of the papers dictate a new title in one of your files, make out the new title immediately. The chore of writing a new title right now is far less than the chore of futilely searching for information filed under a title that doesn't quite fit.

If you don't know what to do with a paper, put it in File Thirteen. In the future, if you wish you had not thrown it away, console yourself with this thought: There is no such thing as irretrievable information. You can get it back from your home office, the office of another company, a government bureau, an associate, a library, or a trade magazine.

These six files -- Administrative, Competitive, Market Data, Technical, Sales Literature and Customer and Prospect, plus File Thirteen -- add up to an easy-to-use and useful system. It achieves a happy balance between having everything you need when and where you need it and a minimum expenditure of time handling the paperwork required for that purpose.

This paper handling system results in at least three benefits with far-reaching impact on your income:

1. It creates more time for selling (or for recreation) by handling each piece of paper just once.
2. It gives you all the information you need at the time and place you need it.
3. It puts you in command of your paperwork instead of vice versa, enabling you always to be up-to-date with your mind free of unresolved problems and the tensions of postponed decisions.

Beginning and Ending a Day

Your day starts the night before in your office, home, or hotel room. Some salespeople clean up the day's work before they eat and prepare for the next day after dinner. Let's base the discussion on this practice -- you have now finished dinner.

You know from prior planning which customers and prospects you will call on tomorrow. Here are five preparatory steps:

1. Review the file folders for each of these customers. Pay particular attention to the Customer Data Sheet and the Sales Record Sheet. Make mental or written notes of company and personal facts. Make sure you have the current order status.
2. In a notebook, or on a separate index card, list the several items you wish to take up on each visit. Don't hesitate to refer to your notes during the sales call. The customer will award you merit points because you thought enough of him to prepare for this call.
3. Review the information in your technical file on

each product you plan to discuss. Don't try to memorize it -- just be sure you know the information you have and can refer to it to support your proposal.

4. Look at your Competitive File and pull out literature you may need.

5. From your Sales Literature File remove the literature you expect to leave with the customer, highlight the portions relevant to this customer and slip it into his file folder.

When you have reviewed the file of each customer, made notes of the agenda for each call, checked the technical information, selected the sales literature, and seen what competitive information is available, if needed, you are ready for your calls tomorrow. You have prepared for a day of satisfying results.

As a salesperson, you are not paid for keeping orderly files or for carefully planning your calls. This organization, however, pays off in increased sales and more satisfied customers. It is for this that you are paid.

Back in your hotel room or office at the end of the day, before dinner, complete the day's work with these steps:

1. Dictate, type or write call reports, if they are needed.

2. Dictate, type or write post-visit letters to your customers where the situation calls for immediate follow-up.

3. Enter new information and summarize your calls on each Customer Data Sheet.

4. Clean out the customer file folders by throwing

away letters, call reports, notes, and other papers you no longer need.

5. Put back in your files the documents and folders you withdrew for that day and then go to dinner -- you will enjoy it more knowing the work of your selling day is behind you.

Call Agenda

In the section above I suggested you may want to write notes for the call on each customer -- items you will cover during each call the next day.

Sometimes when I have proposed the use of a call agenda card, the reaction has been, "Not me! Not on your life! I don't want customers to think I can't remember what I wanted to talk about."

One answer to this objection is: you don't have to let customers see the agenda. A better answer is this: You can add to all the other benefits of the call agenda the admiration you will earn from customers when they see your serious approach to their business by your use of written notes.

What are the virtues of the written call agenda? There are several. It helps eliminate three irritations most salespeople encounter time and again in sales calls -- often enough to be a nuisance, though they may not destroy the call:

1. You forget. How many times as you were driving away from a call did you ruefully realize you forgot to take up an item you had wanted to discuss? A brief outline on the call agenda card gives you a check list you can refer to during the visit and

ensures against omitting a topic. It is easier to think through all you want to cover before you're in front of customers than it is when you're with them.

2. The buyers cut you short. This is another common problem. Customers cut short your interview before you have covered all the subjects. They do hear you through the first item you introduce, but either won't let you bring up additional topics or are so impatient or inattentive that continuing the discussion is useless. How do you forestall this?

Let's say you have been selling Product X to this customer. Today, in addition to talking about that product you want to introduce another application of it and also talk about a new product. The buyers assume you will concentrate on Product X, as on your previous visits. They hear you out, and though they had not expected the story on the additional application, their attention continues as you describe it.

As you draw to the close, they naturally assume you are about to wind up the interview and leave. If instead you say, "Now I'd like to talk to you about a new product," you throw them off balance and make them uneasy. You haven't prepared them for that. Even if they agree to listen, the chances are there will be a trace of annoyance behind the tolerance.

On the other hand, if at the outset of the call you inform the buyers of all the topics you have in mind, you prepare them to hear you through to the end. They will appreciate your courtesy and will look forward with special interest to your story about the new product after your discussion of Product X. If they should veto granting you more time for the new product, you have, at least, left the option in their hands without irritating them.

3. You forget, again. In writing your call reports, have you ever forgotten to put in some information? If you are like me, it has happened more than once. The call agenda card helps alleviate this problem. After the call, you have in front of you, on the card, an outline for your call report. It makes it easy to write a complete, satisfying report.

A call agenda might be written on an index card or simply on a piece of paper. Whatever form, it should be convenient to use.

How visible is the agenda? You may vary its use from call to call. You might keep it in your pocket during most of the call taking it out only near the end, while saying, "Lets see. Did we cover all the topics I wanted to get into today?" Or, you might open the visit by placing it in front of the customer while saying, "Here are a few items I'd like to talk over with you today."

I knew a sales representative who used the call agenda card religiously and sold more product because of it. Her customers admired her organization and her efficient use of their time. When she arrived in a buyer's office, after opening amenities, she opened her portfolio notebook, pulled out her neatly hand-printed agenda, laid it in front of the customer and said, "Here is a list of topics I'd like to take up with you today. What items would you like to add to the list?"

Following this technique both the sales representative

and the buyer had agreed, at the very beginning, on the agenda for their meeting. There were no surprises on either side and the buyer was prepared to participate to the end -- there was never an early termination before she completed all she wanted to do and say.

Furthermore, by inviting the buyer to add to the agenda, whether it was done or not, the invitation turned the agenda into a mutual one that both parties created and both parties had equal interest in seeing completed. It was a master stroke of making the customer a partner in the sale long before anyone had invented partnership selling.

The call agenda card is a simple self-produced sales aid that will pay you large dividends as it:

- helps you remember
- conditions the customers to hear your entire story
- makes the customers partners in your sales call
- pays your customers a genuine, sincere compliment -- it is visual evidence you thought enough of them to think through and organize the call in advance
- makes it easier to write a complete call report.

If you have never used a call agenda card, try it. Print it neatly, place it in front of the buyer and proceed with the sales call. You'll become a convert as your sales grow beyond expectations.

Planned Routing

You now have well organized files, handle paperwork quickly and easily and know how to prepare for each call. What else is there to organizing for better selling? What about knowing how often to make those sales calls and when to make them?

If your planned routing boils down to, "seeing all my customers once every two months," you could be making better use of your time. You are seeing low potential customers more than you can afford to and not devoting enough time to the high-potential customers.

Two figures you should use as guidelines in allocating your time are:

1. average dollars per day you need to reach your sales goal
2. number of days you can afford to spend with each customer and prospective customer.

Both are simple arithmetical calculations.

$$\frac{\text{Dollar Sales Goal}}{\text{Number of work days per year}} = \text{Average Dollars per day}$$

$$\frac{\text{Dollar Potential Customer A}}{\text{Average Dollars per Day}} = \text{Work days for Customer A}$$

If you sell several products, it may pay to calculate the number of days you can afford to devote to any one product. If you forecast Product X to contribute N dollars to your total sales goal, this product should receive a proportionate amount of your time and not more.

$$\frac{\text{N Dollars for Product X}}{\text{Average Dollars per Day}} = \text{Number of Work Days for Product X}$$

Let's assume your territory has the potential to produce $1,000,000 in annual gross sales within a short time. Allowing 240 working days a year, this amounts to $4,167 per day. At this rate a customer with actual or potential purchases of $40,000 should get about 10 days of your time and one with $2,000, one-half day a year.

If the length of each sales call is about the same, you can carry out the calculation to show the approximate dollars you must produce on each visit. To reach your goal of $1,000,000 you must produce $695 on each call when making six calls a day 240 days a year.

Of course, there are modifying factors and you must temper the rigidity of any formula to your intelligent discretion. It does not necessarily require ten times the hours to produce $100,000 in sales as it does $10,000. Nor can you reason that it takes the same number of hours to maintain a given dollar volume on an established product as it does to reach the same level on a new product.

However, unless you develop some method of controlling the relationship of time to sales revenue, you will never reach your goals. If you do not plan your time with customers in a rough proportion to their purchasing power, you will end up with actual sales less than your goal and less than you could have attained.

The Planned Routing form on page 158 is one method of setting both the route and the frequency of customer calls. You list the customers and prospects in geographic order along efficient travel routes. You record the annual potential, either in dollars, or some other common unit, in the column on the right. Using the calculations worked out above, you determine the number of calls per year on each customer and schedule those calls in the 12 trip columns on the left side of the form.

You can show calls you will make by a slash mark (/)

Planned Routing   Trip Area _____

CUSTOMERS & PROSPECTS

TRIPS

JAN	FEB	MAR	APR	MAY	JUN	JUL	AUG	SEP	OCT	NOV	DEC	CITY	NAME	Potential

and after they are made you can cross slash (X). Don't fudge the data -- no one but you sees this Planned Routing sheet, anyway. If you missed intended calls, it will be useful to know that.

In some businesses you will schedule your calls through the year at equally spaced intervals. In other businesses seasonal considerations may dictate unequal spacing. In either case you will apply dollar, or other unit, guidelines. You may want to modify the guidelines in consideration of unique factors applying to certain customers.

Once you fill in the monthly trips for each trip area, add the columns to adjust imbalances in the yearly travel. For example, if the additions disclose the following calls for a particular trip area

Jan	Feb	Mar	Apr	May	Jun
28	5	18	30	3	26

you would move the five in February to March and the three in May to June leaving February and May void for that particular trip area.

A trip area is any convenient subdivision of your territory. It is not a necessary feature of planned routing, but it does simplify planned routing, particularly if you can lay out each trip area as a four to five day work period.

Let's assume you divide your territory into four trip areas of approximately equal number of days. You have filled out the Planned Routing sheets for each trip area, added the columns for each month and made adjustments to avoid isolated visits into an area. We also might assume trip areas A, B, and C, being metropolitan areas, require enough calls to justify monthly trips, while area D may not include large accounts. You can cover area D with a six-week frequency. Now you can write an annual schedule as shown on page 161.

Open weeks or open days in the schedule are necessary to take care of unpredictable developments. A schedule with no flexibility never works for long. You must have some empty spaces to absorb expansion or to accommodate sudden events. If nothing comes up, you can always use the time for cold calls.

It is highly probable the customers in each trip area will vary in potential, requiring twelve, eight, six, four, or two calls per year, according to their dollar importance. Therefore, you will not see every customer every time you are in the trip area. You will balance the calls within the trip area so that the number of calls will add up to about one week's work.

What do you do about the isolated customer in trip area D who needs and deserves attention more than once every six weeks? Or, what do you do about the large customer in trip area A who needs service more than once a month. You can set aside a day or a half-day to see these customers as frequently as the situation demands. Their business is worth this extra time.

Or, you might substitute the telephone for the required extra calls. If telephoning is to be a regular part of the call pattern, you can map it out on the Planned Routing sheet the same as personal visits. You can use a special symbol to flag the planned call as a telephone call.

Once you have done the planned routing for your territory, barring major upheavals, it will be good for several years. It is easy to insert new accounts into the plan and withdraw others. You will never have to wonder where you are going next nor whether you are giving your

ANNUAL TRIP SCHEDULE

Week		Trip Area	Week		Trip Area
JAN	4	A	JUL	5	A
	11	B		12	B
	18	C		19	D
	25	D		26	C
FEB	1	A	AUG	2	A
	8	Open		9	B
	15	B		16	Vacation
	22	C		23	Vacation
				30	C
MAR	1	A	SEP	6	A
	8	D		13	D
	15	B		20	B
	22	C		27	C
	29	A			
APR	5	Open	OCT	4	A
	12	B		11	Open
	19	D		18	B
	26	C		25	C
MAY	3	A	NOV	1	D
	10	B		8	A
	17	Open		15	B
	24	C		22	C
	31	D		29	Open
JUN	7	A	DEC	6	A
	14	B		13	D
	21	C		20	B
	28	Open		27	C

customers the attention their business deserves. Your Planned Routing sheets lead you to:

- see and call customers and prospective customers at the frequency their business with you justifies
- at the time most appropriate
- in efficient travel patterns.

Organization Summed Up

Organizing for better selling requires no expensive equipment. Even if most of your files are on your computer, all you need are some file folders, loose-leaf ring binders and divider tabs, and a wastebasket. And you need a few forms -- Customer Data, Sales Record and Planned Routing. You don't even have to have printed forms. A lined pad with a few hand-drawn lines will do. You also need two or three covered boxes to hold the files.

Organization involves no one but you. You don't need the help of a file clerk, advertising people, product managers, nor your sales manager -- not anyone else. It's your job all the way.

The former head purchasing agent for DuPont had this to say about the salespeople who called on him and his staff:

"The two greatest faults our buyers find with the sales representatives who call on us are their lack of preparation and their lack of organization. They come to see us because we are buying something their company makes. Their approach and their attitude seems to be one of just hoping an order might fall into their lap. Sometimes they do get an order, but not because of anything the salesperson did."

This chapter was written to help you organize and make it easier for you to ask for and get the order. I know from personal experience and the experience of many successful professionals that these ideas work. If you have the desire to start and the self-discipline to maintain organization in your selling efforts, you will reach a higher level of performance, create more satisfied customers, and increase your income.

- Your selling will improve because it is organized.
- It will satisfy you more because the results will be better.
- And, it will be more fun -- the more skill one develops in any pursuit the greater the pleasure in doing it.

CHAPTER 6

IT ALL ADDS UP

*"When love and skill work together, expect a
masterpiece."*
Frank Petrini, 1900-1994

If you were looking for one dramatic revelation to the
question, "What Makes Winners Win?", you didn't find it.
Success in selling is the result of many small victories; the
culmination of doing a multitude of little things right.

Selling, like other professions, requires continuing
attention to skills and knowledge to deliver competent
performance. As a salesperson, commit yourself to lifelong
learning, honing your skills in these five areas:

- Technical knowledge
- Sincere interest in people
- Customer focused selling
- Drive to contact many customers and prospects
- Organization

and your sales, delighted customers, and fulfillment will
have no limits. It all adds up one brick after the other until
you have built a mansion within yourself. Nothing or no
one can top you. It is a very satisfying feeling.

CHAPTER 7

THE FINAL TOUCH

Several years ago I was having lunch with two associates. We were all watching what we ate. It was our usual practice to skip dessert, especially at lunch time.

In most cases, passing up dessert is easily done. Most servers, as they pick up the plates, will simply say, "Will there be anything else?" It is easy to say "No." A small minority will ask, "Would you enjoy some dessert today?" To this query you can usually get by comfortably by smiling and saying, "No thank you" or "Yes, I'd enjoy some dessert, but I'm going to resist today." It is a rare server, indeed, who will say something more.

That day, our waitress turned out to be a member of that rare, select group. When she had completed clearing our table of the main course, she came back to the table with order pad in hand, her pen poised, and said, "We have delicious cherry cobbler today. We make it ourselves. Can I bring three?" There was something about the way she said it that make you think to yourself, "You can't be a heel and refuse an offer like that." The three of us looked at each other and almost simultaneously replied, "Okay, bring three."

As she went for the cobbler we, of course, commented on that unaccustomed bit of good salesmanship. By mentioning a specific dessert in an enticing way she had made a sale which, otherwise, would never have been made. But, she wasn't finished yet.

When our salesperson, the waitress, returned with the three orders of cherry cobbler, she said, as she placed them in front of us, "This looks especially nice today. I know you will enjoy it." That did it! That was the final touch – the stroke that was not necessary but which turned a work of art into a masterpiece.

It is, indeed, a sound and valuable selling technique to congratulate customers on the wisdom of their buying decision.

"You will enjoy years of satisfaction with this machine."

"Your associates are going to be more than pleased when they see what you have done."

"Just think what you're going to do with the savings you will realize with this new process."

"Congratulations, you are going to be very happy with your decision."

This is the final touch that puts the golden seal of professionalism on the sale.

You, too, made a good decision when you bought and committed to reading **WHAT MAKES WINNERS WIN?** If you have received only one new idea from this book, you'll get back your investment of time and money many times over – you will, that is, if you put your new idea into practice.

Why not start now?

Throughout this book you saw quotations by Frank Petrini. They are from *The Proverbs Of Frank Petrini*, published by R&E Publishers, Inc., PO Box 2008, Saratoga, CA 95070; 800-243-9329. Other quotations not attributed to a specific source came from Bartletts Familiar Quotations, 15th edition.

The Author

Charles W. Hitzemann is the founder of Positive Growth International. Chuck designs and delivers workshops on sales, marketing, leadership, and strategic planning. He is a personal coach for sales representatives and sales managers. Prior to founding PGI in 1993, his sales and marketing career with the DuPont Company included assignments throughout the United States and Europe. He represented DuPont as lobbyist to the United States Congress and was the first recipient of the DuPont Corporate Marketing Excellence Award.

For information about workshops, coaching, and consulting services, contact:

Positive Growth International
P.O. Box 725
Smith Mountain Lake
Wirtz, Virginia 24184-0725